Work, Play, and Type

Work, Play, and Type

Achieving Balance in Your Life

Judith A. Provost

CPP Books

Palo Alto, California

A Division of Consulting Psychologists Press, Inc.

96 95 94 93   10 9 8 7 6 5 4 3

Library of Congress Cataloging-in-Publication Data
Provost, Judith A., 1942–
        Work, play, and type: achieving balance in your life / Judith A. Provost.
                p.   cm.
        Includes bibliographical references.
        ISBN 0-89106-040-5
        1. Work—Psychological aspects. 2. Leisure—Psychological aspects. 3. Play—Psychological aspects. 4. Typology (Psychology) 5. Myers-Briggs Type Indicator. I. Title
        BF481.P78   1990
        158—dc20   90-39918
                                                                     CIP

Printed in the United States of America

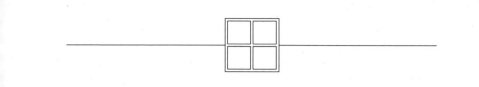

*To all those who have shared with me
the joys of play and laughter*

Contents

Preface ix

**Chapter 1
The Important Ideas 1**
    A Cultural Perspective 3
    Intrinsic Rewards 4
    Adult Development 5

**Chapter 2
Life Stages and Individual Differences 8**
    Developmental Stages 8
    Jung and Personality 10
    Definitions of the Preferences 15
    The Sixteen Combinations of Types 19

**Chapter 3
What Is Adult Play? 25**
    Definitions of Leisure 25
    The Flow Experience 26
    Play as Stimulation 29
    Personality Development Through Play 31

**Chapter 4
Play and Type 39**
    Life Stages, Age, and Needs 40
    Compensatory Leisure and Needs 40
    Personality and Needs Satisfaction 41
    Leisure Styles of the Sixteen Types 47

Chapter 5
Finding Play at Work 55
    Sensing 56
    Intuition 56
    Thinking 57
    Feeling 58
    The Flow Experience at Work 59

Chapter 6
Balancing Work and Play 64
    Balance 64
    Scripts or Archetypes 65
    Rhythms of Work and Play 67
    Real People and Balance 69
    Challenges to Balance 71

Chapter 7
Balancing Work and Play in Relationships 75
    Work, Play, and Couples 75
    The Sixteen Types 81
    Sex as Play 84
    Couples Summary 86
    Work, Play, and Families 86

Chapter 8
Making Changes in the Work and Play Balance 92
    Assertiveness 92
    Taking Responsibility 97
    Positive and Negative Thinking 98
    Imagery 102
    Time Management 107
    Learning from Other Types 109
    Some Final Comments on Change 110

Notes 115
Further Readings 116

Preface

Both in my work as a psychotherapist and consultant and in my personal life, I have encountered many individuals who feel their lives are out of balance and unsatisfying. For more than fifteen years of applying psychological type in both therapy and consulting, I have observed striking variations in the ways different people approach work and play. I wrote this book with the goal of inspiring you to evaluate your own lifestyle and to consider new directions.

This book examines work and how it limits or shapes leisure and affects balance or burnout in people's lives. The emphasis of the book, however, is on play because play is so often neglected by adults in this society.

To achieve balance through work and play, you should first understand something of your own psychology. Thus the first chapter presents information from a Jungian perspective on adult development and personality differences. Next, a way of assessing personality type using the *Myers-Briggs Type Indicator*® (MBTI™) is explained to help you estimate your type. This information is then applied to work and play issues for individuals, relationships, and families. The last chapter includes strategies for effecting lifestyle changes.

Each chapter ends with a section called "Think About," which provides questions designed to provoke reflection about aspects of your own life. These questions help to personalize the ideas in this book and to promote discussion.

I want to emphasize that I do not believe that there is only one way to balance work and play. Individual differences and life circumstances create an infinite number of possible satisfying lifestyles. My hope is that each of you will discover and achieve a work and play balance that is right for you.

Chapter 1

The Important Ideas

Think back to your earliest recollection of play as a child. Do you find that you smile quietly to yourself, perhaps because the thought touches a pleasant chord within? Now think of a time somewhat later—perhaps you were ten or maybe fourteen—when you looked at the adults around you and felt sorry for them because they didn't get to play any more. Do you remember thinking of adults as intimidating, serious beings who had given up fun to go to work? Many adolescents and college students drag their feet through school because they don't want to become that kind of adult. But perhaps you were lucky enough as a child to have some exciting, healthy adult role models, people who were successful in their work *and* also seemed to have fun. Chances are they were playful adults who had a sense of humor.

Now think back to your earliest perceptions of the word *work*. Did you associate this word with chores, such as mowing the lawn or emptying the trash? If you did, then this word might connote an imposed, unappealing, and tedious activity, which if left incomplete brings negative consequences—say, punishment. Or perhaps the word *work* was associated with a parent walking out the door each morning, dressed in a suit and carrying a briefcase. This word may have had a mysterious quality since it was difficult for you to know what your parent really did all day long.

Whatever your specific memories, your experiences have probably caused you to associate play with childhood and work with adulthood. These associations are accompanied by deep feelings and values.

1

We are living in a time when we get mixed or contradic-
tory messages about work and play from our relatives,
employers, government, friends, and from the media. Such
messages include:

- "You are what you do."

- "You are judged by what you acquire—house,
  car, money, and real estate."

- "The American dream is to work only long
  enough to accumulate wealth, then you can retire
  early, travel, be a person of leisure, or live off
  your investments."

- "The successful person can leave work to go
  hang-gliding, play tennis, or hang out with
  friends."

It is no coincidence that several recent American films
have addressed the theme of children and adults exchanging
bodies and lives. In the most successful of these films, *Big*, a
young boy wishes to be "big" and suddenly finds himself in
a thirty-year-old body. Now he has to go to work, but he does
so in a playful, outrageous way. Films like this, though frivo-
lous on the surface, deal with serious issues, such as the loss
of imagination, freedom, and sense of fun in many adult
lives.

But adult play is valuable, and its value rests on these
four premises:

- You can reach your fullest potential through expression and development in *both* work and play.

- Because of differences in personality, individuals
  vary in their attitudes, behavior, needs, and values
  in relation to work and play.

- You can consciously strive to create a balance
  between work and play in your life, which helps
  to preserve physical and mental health and to
  prevent burnout or stagnation.

- Because the extrinsic rewards of work, such as money, goods, and status, are limited, we should develop leisure activities that can provide intrinsic rewards.

A Cultural Perspective

Current attitudes toward work and play often show the influences of early Western philosophers, theologians, and economists. John Stuart Mill, an English philosopher and economist who was a leader of the 19th-century utilitarian movement, claimed that only useful activity was valuable, meaningful, and moral; value was based purely on utility. Max Weber, a German sociologist and economist, wrote about the emergence of the Puritan work ethic that followed the Protestant Reformation. John Calvin and other theologians gradually brought about the association of hard work with virtue. Prior to the Reformation, work had been considered a means to survive and obtain essential goods, but the new ethic gave work a much higher purpose—spiritual salvation. These beliefs about work are one of the underpinnings of capitalism and the American economy. It is no wonder that these beliefs continue to influence us.

In the postindustrial society, scientific and human technology has given us the machinery and social structures to reduce our physical labor and theoretically free us for more leisure. Yet many adults still perceive meaning and value as inherent only in work. The new generation of professionals works longer hours than the previous generation to achieve desired status and material goals. A Harris poll[1] conducted in 1988 reported a decline in Americans' leisure time by one third during the past fifteen years. Harris attributes this decline in part to dual-career marriages and increased white-collar jobs that require more than a 40-hour work week.

Usually we think of *work* as activity for which there is remuneration or some other extrinsic reward, such as academic grades. Work tends to focus on outcomes, products, goods, or services. *Leisure,* on the other hand, is free time not allocated to work or survival. Besides thinking of leisure in relation to time, we use the terms *leisure* and *play* interchangeably in reference to activities chosen freely for their intrinsic value. Leisure and play, unlike work, tend not to focus on productivity and utility.

Intrinsic Rewards

Traditionally, most people work for extrinsic rewards—incomes, cars, houses, and status. Mihaly Csikszentmihalyi, in his pioneering work *Beyond Boredom and Anxiety: The Experience of Play in Work and Games,* pointed out that because resources in our society are limited, it is dangerous for us to rely only on extrinsic rewards. He warned, "When a social system learns to rely exclusively on extrinsic rewards, it creates alienation among its members, and it places a drain on material resources which eventually may prove fatal."[2] As the world population increases and economic conditions fluctuate, we must learn to rely more on intrinsic rewards, such as the joy of simply performing an activity, meeting an intellectual challenge, or attaining a feeling of transcendence. Intrinsic rewards are most easily found in play experiences, although some individuals are able to find them in their work experiences.

Csikszentmihalyi also suggested that certain personalities may be more able than others to incorporate intrinsic rewards into their lives. Certain personality types do seem to find intrinsic rewards more easily, yet all types of people—through self-knowledge and awareness—are capable of restructuring their lives to yield more intrinsic rewards. Intrinsic rewards can bring happiness and satisfaction within the individual's control, whereas extrinsic rewards depend on external circumstances that are often beyond our control.

Adult Development

We can easily see the value of play in children's growth and development. Developmental psychologists, however, have demonstrated that growth does not end with the passage from childhood to adulthood. Thus, play, in addition to work, can be a way for adults to continue their growth and development.

Current thinking about adult development has been greatly influenced by the brilliant work of Swiss psychiatrist Carl Jung. From clinical observations, he constructed a theory about the process of personality development over a lifetime which he called *individuation*. Although we are all born with essentially the same basic mental processes, we individuate over time and develop a unique sense of self. This individuation involves developing certain preferences. An analogy can be drawn with our preference for using one hand or the other; although capable of using either hand, we find the preferred hand more comfortable. These preferences, called *psychological types*, can be encouraged or discouraged from developing and being expressed as a result of environmental factors.

Jung's concepts of individuation and psychological types underlie three of the premises mentioned earlier:

- Psychological type reaches its potential through expression and development in both work and play.

- People who have different psychological types have different attitudes, needs, and values in relation to work and play, and this is reflected in their differing behaviors.

- Each type will benefit from finding a balance between work and play that meets the needs of that type.

This book examines how different psychological types, as described by Jung and measured by the *Myers-Briggs Type Indicator*® (MBTI™), can effect appropriate work and play choices that will lead to a satisfying balance.

Think About ...

1. What cultural attitudes and values do you hold about the importance of work and play?

2. Where did your attitudes about work and play come from? Parents? Church? Personal experience?

3. Have your attitudes about work and play changed over time? If so, how?

4. Do you think you make good use of leisure opportunities? If not, why not?

5. Do you see play and leisure as a way to balance your work life? If so, how?

Chapter 2

Life Stages and
Individual Differences

To look at the nature of work and play in adult life, we must consider life stages and personality. The old saying, "Different strokes for different folks," suggests that individuals differ in personality, needs, values, and interests. Naturally these individual differences will affect work and play. Life stages are important because our needs for work and play change as we pass from childhood to retirement.

Developmental Stages

Developmental theorists such as Erikson and Havighurst identify developmental stages, each associated with certain needs and tasks. These stages begin at birth and span the life of the individual; each stage builds on the previous stage. A stage does not truly end until the specific tasks of that stage have been successfully completed. If not completed, the individual will have difficulty continuing to develop; incomplete life tasks will have to be dealt with at some future time. Developmental stages have a universal sequence, although they may vary in length and time of onset. For example, the adolescent stage, as Erikson conceived it, is one where individuals resolve issues relevant to identity and role. This means that teenagers, for example, must discover how they resemble and differ from family and peers and become comfortable with themselves as young men or women. They must also identify their own values, strengths, and weaknesses and choose specific roles in society. Young people who move into the subsequent stage of early adulthood without successfully completing these tasks are likely to have difficulties later.

Work and play assume varying significance and emphasis in each of the life stages. Childhood play is the vehicle for the development of trust, autonomy, and initiative. It also allows children to develop motor, intellectual, and social skills. Such activities as playing "house," "doctor," and "librarian" prepare children for adult life and work and constitute a rehearsal for future roles. Competition and team cooperation in sports prepare children for the adult versions of these in the workplace. Children may be introduced to work through household chores and assigned tasks, and from this introduction derive a sense of competence and confidence.

In adolescence, play is a means of developing skills further and exploring identity—whether in organized sports, hobbies, social activities, or more personal pursuits. Play is emphasized less than in childhood, yet it is still crucial. Work, in the form of academic effort and employment, is also an important means of development. School success becomes tied to future career success, and part-time jobs provide some spending money and personal freedom. Some adolescents may prematurely stop playing to focus on work because of dysfunctional family or life circumstances. For example, if a parent were to become severely depressed or ill, a teenager may assume the parent role in the family, running the household, caring for younger siblings, and holding a job in addition to school—leaving no time for play. Many adults who have prematurely abrogated play in adolescence must, at some point, rediscover the child or playful self within so that they can be healthy and function fully.

Young adulthood usually continues the focus on school and career development. The emphasis shifts away from play, yet play continues to provide opportunities for completion of the Eriksonian stage of developing intimacy. Young adult and middle adult stages center on career, family, leisure, health, community involvement, and social life. According to Erikson, the developmental effort of middle adulthood is directed toward *generativity*—that is, productivity, leadership, and creativity. In this period, both work and leisure can be sources of generativity, and a balance between the two becomes crucial. In the book *Adult Psychology*, Bischoff notes the value of play to middle-aged people for self-expression, relaxation, catharsis of frustrations and anxieties, and for release of surplus energy. He also notes that people may change their off-the-job interests as they grow older.

In late adulthood and approaching retirement, the focus shifts away from work and toward leisure. Retired persons who have not developed strong leisure interests often experience difficulty making this shift. Without a strongly developed sense of play, they may view their lives as merely the absence of work and feel empty, without identity or meaning in life. Play is crucial to the preservation of mental and physical health. Play can stimulate continued vitality and provide opportunities for further emotional, intellectual, and spiritual development.

Jung and Personality

Jung's theory of individuation and psychological type development further enriches our understanding of the changes we experience during our lives. Jung saw personality as being organized around certain inborn preferences that environment can either foster or inhibit. Jung postulated that everyone has a preferred mental process for *perception*, or finding out about things (Sensing or Intuition), and everyone has a preferred mental process for *judgment*, or coming to

Jung's Mental Functions

Perception Function

Sensing (S) perceiving concretely with the senses	*or*	*iNtuition (N)* perceiving abstractly with intuition

Judgment Function

Thinking (T) evaluating objectively and logically	*or*	*Feeling (F)* evaluating subjectively and personally

conclusions about what's perceived (Thinking or Feeling). These basic mental processes, which Jung called *functions,* can be identified through the *Myers-Briggs Type Indicator,* a questionnaire developed by Katharine Briggs and her daughter, Isabel Briggs Myers, to implement Jung's theory.

Jung stated that each person has a dominant or favorite mental function, either perception or judgment, which serves as "the captain of the ship" to guide the individual through life in a consistent manner. Because it takes the lead, the dominant function has the greatest influence on work, play, and other life choices. In addition, everyone has an auxiliary function, which serves as the "first mate" to the captain and adds balance to the individual's personality. Balance is contributed by the auxiliary function in several ways. If the dominant is a perception function, then the auxiliary will be a judgment function; if the dominant is a judgment function, the auxiliary will be a perception function. There is thus a balance between taking in information and making decisions based on that information. The dominant function will be trusted and emphasized more than the auxiliary, but the auxiliary function will provide balance. Balance does not mean both functions are used equally. An individual favor-

Psychological Balance

	Extraverted Function	Introverted Function
Case #1	Perception (S or N)	with Judgment (T or F)
Case #2	Judgment (T or F)	with Perception (S or N)
Extraverts	the dominant	the auxiliary
Introverts	the auxiliary	the dominant

ing perception but with undeveloped judgment may have trouble making decisions and sticking to them, while an individual favoring judgment but with undeveloped perception may appear rigid and tend to jump to conclusions based on little information.

The other aspect of balance between the dominant and auxiliary functions pertains to the two worlds we must all relate to: the world within ourselves and the world outside ourselves. If we prefer to use our dominant function in the outer world, Jung would say we have a preference for Extraversion. Therefore, to achieve balance, our auxiliary function must be directed to the inner world. We can then say that our dominant function is Extraverted and our auxiliary function is Introverted. Those who prefer to use their dominant function in their inner world are said to have a preference for Introversion; their auxiliary function is used in the outer world and provides the balance. This balance is essential to good adult functioning. An individual without a developed function to use in the outer world would be so introverted as to be alienated from others and in poor contact with the world. The individual without a developed function to use in the inner world would appear superficial and out of touch with internal values and beliefs.

Jung's theory of individuation describes a lifelong process of development of these mental functions. In childhood and early adolescence, almost all energy and attention is naturally given over to the dominant function. People naturally select activities in work and play that exercise their favorite function, just as a right-handed person reacts first with the right hand. Use of this naturally stronger function tends to lead to successful outcomes; this in turn strengthens and encourages further exercise of the dominant function. An environment hostile to the expression of the dominant function may be an exception to this process. Parental disapproval, an educational system emphasizing expression of functions other than the dominant, and other sociocultural influences can force the use of the auxiliary or even of less preferred functions instead of the dominant. For example, some Extraverted, practical-minded parents may view their Introverted, imaginative child as one who lives too much in a fantasy world. Consequently, they may pressure the child to be more extraverted and "realistic" like themselves. Suppression of the dominant function slows down overall development.

When individuals have attained some confidence in expressing their dominant function, they naturally begin to give more attention to developing their auxiliary function through different activities and interests. This usually occurs sometime in adolescence or early adulthood. However, there is no clear timetable for the individuation process. Many teenagers demonstrate in their behavior the imbalance that results from having developed only perception or only judgment. Similarly, some adults—despite their chronological age—have not developed both dominant and auxiliary functions because of environment or circumstances. Without the balance furnished by development of both functions, these adults are more apt to experience difficulty in coping with life.

For example, individuals with a dominant perception function and undeveloped auxiliary judgment may seem like the stereotypical "eternal boy/girl." They may move from job to job, be poor at following through at work, lack persistence when faced with obstacles, and passively wait for opportunities. They generally have trouble being respected or taken seriously. Without auxiliary judgment, these individuals are unable to prioritize and evaluate choices, or make and stick to decisions. Their lives may seem full of play, but often this play is hampered by guilt or conflict because of societal and internal pressures to follow through and succeed. On the other hand, individuals with a dominant judgment function and no balancing auxiliary perception may seem "all work and no play" because they believe that work is never done, and one should not play until work is done. Yet the quality of their work may suffer from quick judgments made without enough information or flexibility. To co-workers they may appear narrow-minded, inflexible, or hard to work with. Without a developed auxiliary function with which to seek information, possibilities, or ideas, they are not open to change.

Once both dominant and auxiliary functions are well developed, individuals are free to explore the less preferred functions in their personalities. This exploration usually begins around midlife or thereafter. It may be that humans have a natural drive to become whole and to claim or express parts of themselves that may have been undeveloped, thwarted, or unconscious. As we mature, we tend to move from being specialists to wanting to be generalists. We are no longer satisfied with the specific roles and functions we originally chose—or had chosen for us. Therefore, our interests naturally move us toward development of the less preferred functions, although we still rely on the dominant and auxiliary for a solid foundation.

The less preferred mental functions are called the *tertiary* and the *inferior* functions. Jung said that these two less preferred functions are in the unconscious and are therefore beyond our conscious control. When we try to use them, the result is often childlike and primitive. Yet in later life, development of these functions brings particular rewards. Many have reported that the cultivation of these less developed functions provides the best opportunities for special satisfaction and spiritual or transcendental experiences. This important idea is discussed more fully later in the book.

Individuation over the lifespan means gradual development of all functions so that we can consciously use the appropriate function called for in a given situation. However, we will never be equally proficient in the use of all four functions. The less preferred functions, for the most part, remain beyond our control and consciousness, and we continue to rely on our dominant and auxiliary to guide us through life.

Definitions of the Preferences

Katharine Briggs and Isabel Briggs Myers developed the *Myers-Briggs Type Indicator* (MBTI) to implement Jung's type theory. The MBTI is one of the most reliable and valid tools for personality assessment and is widely available through counselors, psychologists, teachers, ministers, organizational consultants, and other helping professionals. The MBTI was designed to help people understand themselves and others by helping them to appreciate the different gifts and strengths of each psychological type. Thus, the MBTI is a valuable tool and is commonly used in individual counseling, career and life planning, marriage and family counseling, conflict resolution, organizational consulting and team building, teaching, the ministry and spiritual counseling, and general self-exploration.

The MBTI has four preference scales, so results are reported as four letters, one for each of the four bipolar scales. There are sixteen possible combinations of the eight preferences from the four scales. Each of these sixteen combinations is called a *type*.

As you read the following descriptions of each of the four bipolar scales, try to estimate which of the pair in each of the four scales is your preference. Remember that you probably use all of the eight choices at different times but that you prefer and are more comfortable with four of the eight.

Preferences

Extraversion	or	**I**ntroversion	combine to form the types:
Sensing	or	i**N**tuition	
Thinking	or	**F**eeling	ESTJ, ISFJ,
Judgment	or	**P**erception	ENFP, ISTP, etc.

Extraversion or Introversion: E or I

The first scale is Extraversion–Introversion (E–I). The E–I scale indicates which world individuals prefer to direct their energy toward—the outer world (E) or the inner world (I). This preference suggests where individuals are most likely to direct most of their attention. Extraverts understand the world through acting and reacting to it; they need to externalize things to understand them. They tend to learn by trial and error and generally like a faster pace than Introverts. Extraverts also tend to prefer work involving multiple contacts with people and face-to-face, fast-paced activities. In their play, Extraverts may choose team sports, social events, or opportunities that offer a high level of physical activity and expressiveness.

Introverts understand their world through careful contemplation and prefer not to act or respond without thoughtful consideration. They are internal processors rather than external processors. Introverts generally choose work where they can function independently or one-on-one, with enough time for careful reflection before acting. Their leisure activities tend to be less group-focused and more solitary, such as running, reading, or meditating. It is important, however, not to confuse Jung's and Myers' description of Introverts and Extraverts with the common use of these words. These terms do not refer to degree of sociability. Introverts are just as capable as Extraverts of enjoying friendships and working with people, although they tend to choose their friends more carefully, and they prefer to work with people individually rather than in large groups.

Sensing or Intuition: S or N

The second scale indicates the function you prefer for *perception*—that is, how you take in information and become aware of things, people, events, and ideas. This occurs either through Sensing (S) or Intuition (N). Sensing means finding out about things through the senses and through careful, detailed observation. The sensing function trusts perceptions based on the known, the actual, and the concrete. People with a Sensing preference tend to choose work requiring attention to detail, practical applications of knowledge and skills, and concrete, measurable outcomes. Their leisure may be a further exploration of the senses—for example, through cooking or body building. People who prefer Intuition perceive patterns or relationships among ideas, people, and events. This function trusts perception based on intuitions. One might say that Intuitive types read between the lines rather than confining their attention to the exact words. Intuition is associated with theory, speculation, and possibility and emphasizes the abstract over the concrete, whereas Sensing emphasizes common sense, direct experience, and what is real and verifiable. Sensing, by its very nature, occurs in the here and now, with some attention given to the past and tradition. Intuition, by its speculative nature, is oriented more toward the future and its possibilities. People who prefer Intuition tend to pick work of a less defined, more ambiguous nature, requiring innovative problem solving. Their leisure is likely to focus on novelty, imagination, and discovery—for example, through art classes, reading or writing fiction, or photography.

Thinking or Feeling: T or F

The third scale indicates the preferred *judgment* function. The judgment function describes how you come to conclusions or make decisions about what you have perceived by either Thinking (T) or Feeling (F). Jung and Myers used these terms very differently from the everyday meanings: both

Thinking and Feeling types use certain criteria in arriving at conclusions. Thinking types use objective criteria, and Feeling types use subjective criteria. Here, Thinking means considering pros and cons or consequences, analyzing the information at hand, and coming to a logical choice, decision, or conclusion. People with a Thinking preference often tend to choose work involving analysis of data, logic, or some kind of technology. Their leisure interests might include such activities as tinkering with an old car, playing chess, or reading mysteries.

Feeling, as Jung and Myers mean it, involves weighing personal values and people's reactions: Will there be conflict, harmony, approval, or disapproval? Decisions or conclusions reached by Feeling types may appear to a Thinking type as spontaneous "yes—no," "good—bad" judgments, difficult to justify logically. Individuals with a Feeling preference often choose work in which "reading" other people is essential, whether in persuasion-oriented or service-oriented careers such as teaching or counseling. Their leisure interests might center on personal expression such as music, poetry, or personal interactions with others. Each function, then, has its strengths and its potential blind spots. Those with a Feeling preference often neglect logical reasoning and fail to consider consequences. Those with a Thinking preference often neglect taking other people's reactions—and even their own emotional responses—into account.

Judgment or Perception: J or P

The last scale was created by Briggs and Myers to clarify an aspect of Jung's theory that was implicit in his writings. The Judgment–Perception (J–P) scale indicates whether the individual uses a judgment function (T, Thinking, or F, Feeling) or a perception function (S, Sensing, or N, Intuition) in the outer world. People who have a J for the fourth letter in their type use Judgment in an extraverted way and are often seen as decisive and organized, liking structure and closure. Such people tend to be more attracted to management positions and enjoy working in structured organizations. Their leisure time is usually carefully planned and left until work is completed. People who have a *P* as the fourth letter use Perception in the outer world and are often seen as flexible, spontaneous, open-minded, and uncomfortable with much structure and planning. Perceptive types tend to choose work that allows flexibility and freedom with an element of unpredictability. Their leisure is less planned and may occur spontaneously, even if their work is not finished.

It is important to remember that the MBTI indicates natural preferences—the ways we *prefer* to be. Often, however, we may act differently from our preferences because the situation demands it or because we are not comfortable with using our preferences. We all express each of these eight preferences at different times in different circumstances, but the MBTI tells us which four we prefer to express most of the time.

The Sixteen Combinations of Types

The list below summarizes the four MBTI scales. Try to guess which of these preferences describes you, then read the brief type descriptions for the sixteen combinations in Table 1. (Remember, to accurately identify your type, the MBTI should be administered and interpreted to you by a trained professional.)

- Where is most of your attention and energy directed? Outward (Extraversion) or inward (Introversion)?

- Perception: How do you find out about things? Sensing or Intuition?

Table 1. Brief Descriptions of the Sixteen Types

Sensing Types

	ISTJ	ISFJ
Introverts	Serious, quiet, earn success by concentration and thoroughness. Practical, orderly, matter-of-fact, logical, realistic, and dependable. See to it that everything is well organized. Take responsibility. Make up their own minds as to what should be accomplished and work toward it steadily, regardless of protests or distractions.	Quiet, friendly, responsible, and conscientious. Work devotedly to meet their obligations. Lend stability to any project or group. Thorough, painstaking, accurate. Their interests are usually not technical. Can be patient with necessary details. Loyal, considerate, perceptive, concerned with how other people feel.

	ISTP	ISFP
Introverts	Cool onlookers—quiet, reserved, observing and analyzing life with detached curiosity and unexpected flashes of original humor. Usually interested in cause and effect, how and why mechanical things work, and in organizing facts using logical principles.	Retiring, quietly friendly, sensitive, kind, modest about their abilities. Shun disagreements, do not force their opinions or values on others. Usually do not care to lead but are often loyal followers. Often relaxed about getting things done, because they enjoy the present moment and do not want to spoil it by undue haste or exertion.

	ESTP	ESFP
Extraverts	Good at on-the-spot problem solving. Do not worry, enjoy whatever comes along. Tend to like mechanical things and sports, with friends on the side. Adaptable, tolerant, generally conservative in values. Dislike long explanations. Are best with real things that can be worked, handled, taken apart, or put together.	Outgoing, easygoing, accepting, friendly, enjoy everything and make things more fun for others by their enjoyment. Like sports and making things happen. Know what's going on and join in eagerly. Find remembering facts easier than mastering theories. Are best in situations that need sound common sense and practical ability with people as well as with things.

	ESTJ	ESFJ
Extraverts	Practical, realistic, matter-of-fact, with a natural head for business or mechanics. Not interested in subjects they see no use for, but can apply themselves when necessary. Like to organize and run activities. Make make good administrators, especially if they remember to consider others' feelings and points of view.	Warm-hearted, talkative, popular, conscientious, born cooperators, active committee members. Need harmony and may be good at creating it. Always doing something nice for someone. Work best with encouragement and praise. Main interest is in things that directly and visibly affect people's lives.

Intuitive Types

INFJ	INTJ	
Succeed by perseverance, originality, and desire to do whatever is needed or wanted. Put their best efforts into their work. Quietly forceful, conscientious, concerned for others. Respected for their firm principles. Likely to be honored and followed for their clear convictions as to how best to serve the common good.	Usually have original minds and great drive for their own ideas and purposes. In fields that appeal to them, they have a fine power to organize a job and carry it through with or without help. Skeptical, critical, independent, determined, sometimes stubborn. Must learn to yield less important points in order to win the most important.	Introverts
INFP	INTP	
Full of enthusiasms and loyalties, but seldom talk of these until they know you well. Care about learning, ideas, language, and independent projects of their own. Tend to undertake too much, then somehow get it done. Friendly, but often too absorbed in what they are doing to be sociable. Little concerned with possessions or physical surroundings.	Quiet and reserved. Especially enjoy theoretical or scientific pursuits. Like solving problems with logic and analysis. Usually interested mainly in ideas, with little liking for parties or small talk. Tend to have sharply defined interests. Need careers where some strong interest can be used and useful.	Introverts
ENFP	ENTP	
Warmly enthusiastic, high-spirited, ingenious, imaginative. Able to do almost anything that interests them. Quick with a solution for any difficulty and ready to help anyone with a problem. Often rely on their ability to improvise instead of preparing in advance. Can usually find compelling reasons for whatever they want.	Quick, ingenious, good at many things. Stimulating company, alert, and outspoken. May argue for fun on either side of a question. Resourceful in solving new and challenging problems, but may neglect routine assignments. Apt to turn to one new interest after another. Skillful in finding logical reasons for what they want.	Extraverts
ENFJ	ENTJ	
Responsive and responsible. Generally feel real concern for what others think or want, and try to handle things with due regard for the other person's feelings. Can present a proposal or lead a group discussion with ease and tact. Sociable, popular, sympathetic. Responsive to praise and criticism.	Hearty, frank, decisive, leaders in activities. Usually good in anything that requires reasoning and intelligent talk, such as public speaking. Are usually well informed and enjoy adding to their fund of knowledge. May sometimes appear more positive and confident than their experience in an area warrants.	Extraverts

- Judgment: How do you decide? Thinking or Feeling?

- What is your attitude to the outer world? Judgment or Perception?

If you know, or guess, your type, refer to Table 2 to determine your dominant, auxiliary, and least preferred functions. The table also indicates whether a particular function is extraverted (E) or introverted (I).

Now let's return to the concept of individuation and see how it applies to a specific type. Find ESFJ on both of the tables. A person with ESFJ preferences uses Feeling judgment to deal with the outer world, so the dominant function is Feeling, since the outer world is where Extraverts use their dominant function. The auxiliary function is Sensing, which is introverted, and is used when the individual quietly withdraws to examine Sensing perceptions. In early life, this person would tend to put more energy into expressing the Feeling function—perhaps by being a social organizer and leader at school. In later adolescence or early adulthood, he or she is likely to give more attention to Sensing, and so might enjoy collecting stamps or reading stories about famous people. At midlife, the ESFJ might begin exploring the less developed functions, Thinking and Intuition. This individual might engage the Thinking function by learning to play chess with someone he or she likes. Intuition might be developed by attending foreign films and discussing their meaning with friends, or by joining a museum society and learning about modern art by discussing it with artists, critics, and art enthusiasts.

These sixteen psychological types shape not only the lifestyles people choose, but also their willingness to change at various life stages. Most of us have a clear understanding of the nature of work—but what exactly does play mean for adults?

Table 2. Order of Preferences for Each Type—letters in parentheses indicate extraverted/introverted function.

	ISTJ		ISFJ		INFJ		INTJ	
1. DOMINANT	S	(I)	S	(I)	N	(I)	N	(I)
2. AUXILIARY	T	(E)	F	(E)	F	(E)	T	(E)
3. TERTIARY	F	(E)	T	(E)	T	(E)	F	(E)
4. Least-preferred	N	(E)	N	(E)	S	(E)	S	(E)

	ISTP		ISFP		INFP		INTP	
1. DOMINANT	T	(I)	F	(I)	F	(I)	T	(I)
2. AUXILIARY	S	(E)	S	(E)	N	(E)	N	(E)
3. TERTIARY	N	(E)	N	(E)	S	(E)	S	(E)
4. Least-preferred	F	(E)	T	(E)	T	(E)	F	(E)

	ESTP		ESFP		ENFP		ENTP	
1. DOMINANT	S	(E)	S	(E)	N	(E)	N	(E)
2. AUXILIARY	T	(I)	F	(I)	F	(I)	T	(I)
3. TERTIARY	F	(I)	T	(I)	T	(I)	F	(I)
4. Least-preferred	N	(I)	N	(I)	S	(I)	S	(I)

	ESTJ		ESFJ		ENFJ		ENTJ	
1. DOMINANT	T	(E)	F	(E)	F	(E)	T	(E)
2. AUXILIARY	S	(I)	S	(I)	N	(I)	N	(I)
3. TERTIARY	N	(I)	N	(I)	S	(I)	S	(I)
4. Least-preferred	F	(I)	T	(I)	T	(I)	F	(I)

From *Introduction to Type*. Copyright © 1962, 1970, 1976 by Isabel Briggs Myers. Copyright © 1980, 1987 by Consulting Psychologists Press, Inc.

Think About ...

1. What stage of life are you in, and in what stage of life are the important people in your life?

2. In what ways are your proportions of work and play similar to or different from the proportions of those who are important in your life?

3. What do you consider to be the biggest task or challenge of your current life stage?

4. What memories of satisfying play do you recall from the various life stages: childhood, adolescence, early adulthood, middle years, and after age 50?

5. What four MBTI preferences did you guess were probably descriptive of you?

6. What are some examples of work and play interests and behavior for each of the four preferences you chose?

Chapter 3

What Is Adult Play?

Leisure is free time, not obligated for work or life maintenance, to be used at the discretion of the individual. Thus, we
define leisure in relation to time and work. Play is a subset of
leisure, although Csikszentmihalyi, the research psychologist cited earlier, argues that play can sometimes be found in
work. We usually think of play as voluntary activity that
reflects individual freedom, is nonutilitarian, has intrinsic
rewards, and often is "a state of mind."

Definitions of Leisure

When defined in reference to work, there are two basic kinds
of leisure. One is called *compensatory* leisure or play, through
which individuals meet needs that are not met in their jobs.
An example would be Extraverted types whose jobs require
sitting quietly in an office all day, and who use leisure for
highly physical activities with others—thereby satisfying
needs for social interaction and energy release through activity. Introverted types who are actively engaged with people
all day might choose leisure of a more solitary nature, such
as reading a novel, going on a long walk alone, or taking a
bubble bath with the phone off the hook. Compensatory
leisure allows the Introverts to renew themselves by focusing on their inner world. The other work-related category of

leisure is called *spillover* because those who spend their leisure time in this way carry the same kinds of activities and interests from their work into their leisure. An example of this might be a literature professor whose play activity includes reading more books in his or her field and browsing in bookstores, or a professional baseball player who relaxes by coaching underprivileged children in baseball skills.

The Flow Experience

Csikszentmihalyi does not see a clear distinction between work and play, but rather sees the two as points on a continuum defined by the amount of extrinsic versus intrinsic reward. He is one of several theorists who include in their definition of play the element of intrinsic rewards—for example, good feelings, spiritual well-being, and intellectual or physical stimulation. Work tends to have primarily extrinsic rewards, such as salary or status. Csikszentmihalyi claims, however, that some personalities are capable of restructuring their work environments and changing their conceptions of work so that both intrinsic rewards and what he terms "flow" experiences are possible. These individuals play at work. Csikszentmihalyi further suggests that we are more capable of deriving intrinsic rewards from work as we mature and become more affluent. This idea makes sense, especially in terms of Maslow's hierarchy of needs, which suggests that the individual can move toward self-actualization and satisfaction of more complex needs once basic needs such as food, shelter, and safety have been met.

Csikszentmihalyi goes on to describe what a person in the "flow" experiences: "a unified flowing from one moment to the next, in which he [sic] is in control of his actions, and in which there is little distinction between self and environment, between stimulus and response, or between past, present, and future."[3] Other writers and researchers have described this condition as a transcendental, religious, or peak experience. The individual loses consciousness of self or ego because of complete absorption in the activity. This flow is sometimes experienced by individuals when engaged in leisure activities that stimulate the inferior, or least preferred, functions. For example, a 50-year-old man with INFP preferences may frequently have flow experiences while working with wood in his home shop. His concentration is intense as he uses his less preferred Sensing and Thinking functions to work the wood; this activity calls into play logic, planning, attention to detail, and precision of execution. Woodworking also focuses all his attention on a narrow field chosen not for utilitarian value but for pleasure. These are crucial to the flow experience.

During the flow experience, one is not "spectating" or stepping outside the experience to watch oneself act. In fact, a shift of focus to spectating—such as asking oneself, "How am I doing?"—interrupts the flow experience. Perhaps you can recall experiences of this kind: for example, playing tennis and serving aces almost unconsciously but then double-faulting as soon as you begin thinking about your service technique, or playing the piano beautifully until you remember to check if your fingering is correct. The flow, and the interruption of that flow through spectating, are also a frequent pattern in sexual activity. People who seek counseling for sexual difficulties frequently report spectating behavior in which they self-consciously "freeze" or can't relax, while those who report sexual satisfaction describe losing a sense of self by relaxing and focusing fully on the sensual experience. You may recall a scene in the film *Annie Hall* where Diane Keaton and Woody Allen are trying to make love. An image of Annie floats above the bed, providing a running commentary about Alvie Singer's amorous efforts; she finds herself unable to relax and stop spectating, so the result, of course, is a disaster for them both.

Besides the *loss of self-awareness,* another condition necessary for the flow experience is the presence of *repetitive stimuli*—for example, the even, regular strokes of a swimmer or strides of a long distance runner. Also, narrowing one's *focus of attention* to a few specific stimuli is essential to attaining a flow experience. For example, a dominant Intuitive type may experience flow while hitting tennis balls and focusing on the fuzz and seams of the balls and the sound of the racquet connecting with the ball. In this process, this person is also exercising an inferior Sensing function. Someone else might find similar satisfaction in practicing scales on the piano, running several miles, or practicing calligraphy.

Another essential ingredient of the flow experience is a *balance between ability and the level of challenge within the activity.* Too much challenge in relation to ability leads to frustration; too little challenge leads to boredom. In neither case does the flow experience result. This principle can also be applied to use of the dominant and inferior functions. We can take on much greater challenges with our dominant functions than we can with our inferior ones. This partly explains why leisure activities, without the pressures and evaluation of work, are safer places to explore our inferior function. To stimulate development of our lesser functions, we must carefully select activities that do not overtax these functions beyond our abilities.

Csikszentmihalyi's research focused on individuals engaged in several kinds of activities resulting in frequent flow experiences: rock climbing, championship chess playing, basketball, dancing to rock music, composing music, and performing surgery. He observed a common experience among these subjects, captured by the German term *funktionlust,* meaning "the pleasurable sensation that an organism experiences when it is functioning according to its physical and sensory potential."[4]

Csikszentmihalyi found within these activities two principal characteristics: "exploring the limits of abilities and trying to expand them," and "a feeling of novelty and challenge."[5] He identified two kinds of challenge: (a) the challenge of the unknown, leading to discovery or a solution to some kind of problem (say, as in composing, climbing, or chess), which might appeal to Intuitive types (or dominant Intuitives with auxiliary thinking functions) and (b) "the

Necessary Conditions for "Flow"

- acute concentration on a narrow field
- focus away from self
- repetitive stimuli and activity
- variable, with an open-ended outcome
- ability proportionate to challenge

concrete challenge of competition" (say, as in basketball, which might appeal more to Sensing types).

To summarize, play that results in a flow experience must be completely absorbing, require active participation, be open-ended, and result in pleasurable release from duties associated with work. Flow is a desirable, intrinsic reward of play because feelings of renewal, increased self-confidence, and spiritual growth are generated. The flow experience resembles, in some respects, the altered state of meditation and has similar benefits.

Play as Stimulation

Another researcher of play behavior, M. Ellis, in *Why People Play*, made observations related to intrinsic rewards, stimulation, and challenge, pointing out that play not only is critical to children's development, but also to adult achievement of individuality. Ellis searched for an answer to this question: Why does the child, adult, or animal continue to behave playfully when apparently his or her needs are all satisfied? The explanation he favored combined developmental factors with an arousal-seeking model, which assumes that adults have a need to produce effects in the environment to demonstrate competence, to feel in control, and to experience stimulation for its own sake. Play is thus considered a class of behavior that increases the level of arousal or stimulation.

Ellis' position, that play is an arousal-seeking and developmental activity, can be considered in relation to psychological types. Certain types—the Extraverted Perceptives (ESFP, ESTP, ENFP, and ENTP)—seem to be particularly interested in seeking arousal. Their dominant function is perceptive and extraverted; they constantly look for stimuli in their environments. Sensing types look for activities and experiences that arouse their five senses, as, for example, team sports, social gatherings with interesting people, food and drink, and so forth. Intuitive types look for novel and ever-changing experiences that pique their curiosity and desire for the unique and intriguing, as, for example, conversations with fascinating personalities or attendance at unusual performing arts events. All these types tend to have a high activity level and a high need for stimulation and arousal. If work does not offer these satisfactions, it is crucial that leisure compensate for the lack.

Types with introverted dominant perception (INFJ, INTJ, ISTJ, and ISFJ) are less obvious in their pursuit of stimulation, yet their leisure activities may subtly achieve that purpose. Introverted Sensing types (ISTJ or ISFJ) may choose activities involving collection and organization of many pieces of information or objects, such as keeping track of baseball statistics or collecting antiques. Introverted Intuitive types (INTJ or INFJ) may choose activities that stimulate internal speculation and opportunities to shape new ideas, such as playing chess or reading fiction and theoretical works. With most Introverted Perceptives, the focus is on internal stimulation. Introverts seem to have a lower tolerance for external stimulation than Extraverts and tend to become drained when they must focus energy outside themselves for extended lengths of time. They become energized by turning inward. Extraverts, on the other hand, derive energy by relating to the outer world and may feel their energy depleted if isolated for very long from others or stimulating events.

Types with a dominant Judgment function, either Thinking or Feeling, also seek arousal, but probably not to the extent of most dominant Perceptive types. Their focus is likely to be more on the control dimension of play—exploring their capability to control the environment and master some activity or event. For an ENTJ, for example, play might mean perfecting a particular tennis stroke. For an ESFJ, organizing a party by skillfully managing the people, atmosphere, and food may be satisfying. An ISTP might find satisfaction in mastering the environment of an underwater cave where skills in handling equipment and dealing with dangerous conditions are paramount.

Personality Development Through Play

On the following pages are some examples of play activities for each of the mental functions (S, N, T, F). The examples are particularly relevant where that function is the favorite or dominant for an individual. Children, adolescents, and young adults are likely to engage in activities that express the dominant function. Older adults may choose activities to help develop their less preferred functions.

Play and the Less Preferred Functions

Type development through play takes on new importance during and after midlife when dominant and auxiliary functions are usually well developed. This is a stage in life when new interests and activities can allow development and strengthening of less preferred functions. Play is the best place for such development because it doesn't have the pressure and stress associated with work. Leisure becomes a safe place to experiment with the less preferred functions.

Examples of Play Activities for Each of the Mental Functions

Dominant Sensing types might:

- read stories of famous people and true adventures
- engage in domestic arts such as cooking, sewing, gardening, or interior design
- take pleasure in toys or gadgets with mechanical components
- enjoy taking things apart and putting them back together
- engage in team sports such as basketball, football, and volleyball

Dominant Thinking types might:

- enjoy chess, Japanese go, and other games of logic and strategy
- practice a sport where they can measure their mastery, such as golf, riflery, weightlifting, or track
- engage in competitions such as debating or tennis
- read philosophy or nonfiction

Examples of Play Activities for Each of the Mental Functions

Dominant Intuitive types might:

- read fantasy or other fiction
- engage in imaginative play
- enjoy radio and television programs of an imaginative nature
- play word games and complex board games
- take a special interest in painting, drama, and other artistic activities

Dominant Feeling types might:

- emphasize friendships and enjoy hanging out and talking on the phone
- keep journals or scrap books and write letters
- join social organizations
- engage in noncompetitive sports and games
- read romantic or human interest literature

The satisfaction that results from activities using the less preferred functions are often more intense and exceptional than those involving the dominant function. As adults, we often take the strengths associated with our dominant and auxiliary functions for granted and assume positive outcomes in these areas because they are stronger. With the third and fourth functions, however, such positive outcomes are less certain but can be more gratifying. For example, an ENFP woman described her joy in helping to build a deck in her backyard, which required her to use her least preferred function, Sensing, as she carefully placed and hammered the nails so as not to split the boards. She described the level of concentration it took and her need not to have anyone criticize or rush her. She also attested to a feeling of triumph that was stronger than that felt after success in her more usual endeavors. Other examples of less-preferred functions being used in play and leisure are listed below.

- An ESTJ develops his NF by attending art shows with friends and discussing his reactions to what he saw.

- An ENFP becomes interested in nature photography in which he takes closeups of flower petals and drops of dew.

- An ISTJ takes a psychology course just for fun.

- An ISTP attends small, informal group discussions on abstract topics in which most of the members are Intuitives and each participant shares personal reactions to the ideas.

- An ESFJ reads science fiction, then discusses it with his teenage son.

- An INFJ practices a complicated piano piece that requires painstaking repetition of difficult passages.

- An INFP makes friends who are Thinking types that engage her in analytical debates.

- An ENFJ participates in the technical aspects of building her own house.

- An INTJ takes up the fast-paced, physically intense sport of handball.

- An INTP finds that he likes small, intimate dinners during which friends share their experiences and confidences.

- An ENTP who never had danced as a youth discovers that dancing is a joyful experience.

- An ENTJ decides to go fishing with a friend and takes pleasure in the fact that it doesn't matter whether they catch any fish.

- An ISFJ takes a course in watercolor technique, experimenting with abstracts and landscapes.

- An ISFP tinkers on a home computer with a financial planning software package.

- An ESTP joins the local theater and performs in several Shakespearean productions.

- An ESFP dabbles in parapsychology, reading and attending programs on astrology and numerology.

Jung and other type theorists have speculated that the door to spiritual awareness may be through exercise of the third and fourth functions because these reside in the unconscious, and therein lies the key to our connection to the divine. To embrace and develop these aspects of the self allows some to experience a spiritual awakening. When describing experiences in which they've used the less preferred functions, people often report a sense of transcendence and unity, a blending with nature or humanity, and a loss of a sense of self or ego. Play, then, may include a spiritual dimension. For example, an ESTJ who joined a men's consciousness-raising group and explored his inferior Feeling function through sharing emotions and experiences with others reported "a sense of worship" at these gatherings. A dominant Intuitive reported a sense of "oneness with the ocean and its inhabitants, a sense of the divine in nature" while snorkeling; she used Sensing to focus on breathing, body movement, and the details of the fish and coral around her.

Of course, other factors besides psychological type determine leisure behavior: socioeconomic status, gender, cultural and ethnic orientation, health, and age. These factors interact with type to shape the kinds of leisure activities we enjoy. A good example of gender and type interaction relates to the Thinking–Feeling preference. The majority of men have a Thinking preference, and the majority of women a Feeling preference. Bishoff observed that men often develop "more feminine interests" later in life. Without knowing about type, he was probably identifying the phenomenon of a Thinking type developing the less preferred Feeling function at midlife. Our culture still tends to stereotype certain leisure interests as "masculine" and "feminine." Rohbaugh researched the importance of sports for women and found this play activity to be a release from traditional roles—a "joyous, liberating effect" that enhances self-confidence.[6] Feeling type women, especially, may avoid physical competition and contact sports when young, then may later find this kind of play a way to develop Thinking. Certainly the Feeling woman who has difficulty being assertive because of her concern for harmony can find the competition in sports helpful in developing assertiveness.

This general overview of adult play allows us to look at specific individual needs that can be satisfied through play and how these needs relate to personality differences.

Think About ...

1. Is your leisure primarily compensatory or spillover? Give some examples.

2. Have you ever had a flow experience? Describe the feelings and circumstances.

3. What circumstances and activities could you cultivate to increase your flow experiences?

4. What intrinsic rewards do you receive from play?

5. When you guessed at your dominant function, did you find your leisure interests listed on pages 32 and 33? If not, what activities would you add?

6. What, if any, leisure activities engage your less preferred functions? How do they differ from those associated with your dominant function?

7. Have you ever experienced a spiritual dimension to your leisure or play?

8. How does your gender influence your leisure choices?

9. How do other factors, such as age and economic status, influence your leisure choices?

Chapter 4

Play and Type

Play can satisfy many adult needs. The previous chapter showed how play can provide intrinsic rewards: stimulation, novelty, challenge, control, spiritual exploration, and a harmonious, altered state—the flow experience. Most importantly, play provides a way to express and develop type preferences. Play can also provide a balance to work in two ways—through compensatory activities, or through an extension of work-related interests called spillover leisure.

Specific adult needs are often satisfied through play. Florida State University researchers M. Ragheb and J. Beard[7] identified six categories of needs that can be satisfied through play:

- **Psychological Needs**
  Includes such benefits as enjoyment, a sense of freedom, and intellectual challenge

- **Educational Needs**
  Includes such benefits as making discoveries about the world and gaining self-knowledge and information

- **Social Needs**
  Involves relationships with others, family, and friends

- **Relaxational Needs**
  Allows relief from the stress and tension of daily life

- **Physiological Needs**
  Involves health, physical fitness, weight control, and other aspects of well-being

- **Aesthetic Needs**
  Includes appreciation of and pleasure in beauty
  and good design, not only in the arts, but in nature,
  often experienced as a sense of deep harmony

Life Stages, Age, and Needs

People have varying levels of needs in each of these categories at different life stages. For example, college students
usually have low educational needs related to play, since
education is their basic task during this time of their life.
However, college students do have a high need for relaxational and social leisure. They need both to release the
tension created by academic pressure and to use their free
time to develop social relationships, affiliation, and intimacy. On the other hand, older individuals may place a
higher value on physiological needs because aging makes
health and fitness a priority.

Compensatory Leisure and Needs

These categories of needs help us to think about leisure as a
compensation for work. College students' leisure is one
example. Another example is the individual who works in a
military weapons plant and finds balance in aesthetic leisure, perhaps by collecting art and attending art shows and
museums. A retired person who has always lived and worked
in the same city may seek satisfaction of educational needs
through travel and Elder Hostels.

Personality and Needs Satisfaction

Different personality types may have stronger needs in some of these categories because of their desire to express dominant and auxiliary preferences. For example, the needs in the Psychological category may be felt most strongly by those with preferences for Introversion and Intuition, especially the INFP's and INTP's. These types derive great personal satisfaction from inner discovery through reading, keeping a journal, writing, meditation, and so forth.

Different aspects of the Educational category may appeal to different types. Intuitives may be perpetual students throughout their lifetimes, taking courses and workshops out of curiosity and for fun. Intuitive Feeling types, in particular, will look for educational experiences that emphasize self-knowledge. Sensing types may choose to travel to satisfy their need to learn about the world through direct experience; they may also like reading or taking seminars about real places and things.

Although everyone needs some degree of social satisfaction, the Social needs category appeals most obviously to Extraverts and Feeling types. Extraverts tend to prefer a high level of social interaction with a wide variety of people, while Feeling types, both introverted and extraverted, satisfy affiliative needs through activities centered around people.

Relaxational leisure is best understood in the context of one's psychological type and the lifestyle that best suits that type. One must also consider the level of stress experienced at work. For example, an ESTJ business executive, who must spend high-pressure days making numerous quick decisions, dealing with people, and running from meeting to meeting, may find a strong need for relaxation and leisure in such activities as going for a quiet walk on the beach or just lying in a hammock. Another ESTJ, who must listen attentively all day to the personal problems of her supervisees, might find that a fast, energetic game of racquetball is the best relaxation; she can let off steam after having used her less developed Feeling function so much at work. Using less preferred functions for most of the work day is tiring and stressful. Extraverts tend to have a higher energy level than Introverts—in the sense of need for physical activity—and thus may find relaxation in very physical and active leisure. Those Intuitives who live in their heads all day may achieve relaxation through Sensing and physical leisure that reconnects them, as it were, to their bodies. To summarize the relationship of relaxational leisure to psychological types and their work, we could say if people work in jobs that call greatly upon their less preferred functions, they probably have a stronger need for relaxational leisure than those whose work primarily uses their favored functions. Relaxational activities therefore provide a balance.

Physiological leisure will appeal more to certain types than to others. ENFP's and ENTP's, especially, as well as the dominant introverted Intuitives, tend to be less aware of their bodies because their inferior function is Sensing. Their attention is given more to ideas and to possibilities far removed from bodily sensations or conditions in the here and now. They are more likely to neglect their bodies until middle age or later when they have developed their Sensing function and learned from the consequences of past neglect. Sensing types, on the other hand, attend more readily to health, fitness, weight, and related issues and will probably be more consistent in their physiological leisure behavior. If they are SJ types, they will probably be very self-disciplined in sticking to exercise programs— especially when compared to ENFP's and ENTP's, who tend to be sporadic in their physiological leisure efforts; they may be enthusiastic, almost evangelistic, about an activity at first, but then lose interest after a short time. SJ types, however, may deny themselves physiological activity, despite their interest in it, because of their strong sense of responsibility to work and to others, believing that they cannot participate until all their responsibilities have been fulfilled.

Aesthetic needs can be met through a variety of activities appealing to different types. Of all sixteen, the Introverted Feeling types (INFP, ISFP) probably have the strongest need for harmony in their environment and may thus be particularly motivated to pursue art, design, music, dance, and related activities. An ISTJ may satisfy aesthetic needs through careful construction of a model, sculpture, or other object that has pleasing symmetry, order, and economy of parts.

Table 3 presents a summary of trends in type for each of the six leisure needs. Remember that all types have all six leisure needs in differing degrees, depending on their stages of development and their lifestyles.

If the preceding table seems too neat in its matching of type with play activity, it is crucial to realize that one cannot determine *why* someone engages in a play activity merely by identifying the activity. One must look at what needs are met by the activity and how the individual approaches it. Type is a great influence; for example, an ENFP may play tennis for relaxation and social satisfaction, choosing only people he or she enjoys playing with and finding great tension release in simply hitting the ball and running around on the tennis court. An INTJ, on the other hand, may approach tennis less as a game than as a test of mastery and personal control. Each time he or she plays, the goal is to play a little better than before, measuring improvement carefully. In this case, primarily psychological needs, rather than social or relaxational needs, are being met by the same leisure activity.

Intuitive Thinking (NT) types place high priority on mastery and competence in all that they do. Some may argue that when NT types bring issues of mastery and competence to their play, they can be overly self-critical if they don't live up to their own standards: Playing, then, becomes similar to work. Of course, this observation may just be the bias of non-NT types making judgments based on their own value systems. This is a good example of how, when applying type theory, we should be careful not to evaluate the quality of others' leisure or play on the basis of our own type's biases

Table 3. The Relationship of Type to the Six Leisure Needs

Leisure Need	Predominant Type	
Psychological (intellectual challenge and freedom, self-confidence, etc.)	IN, NP	individualistic pursuit of ideas, e.g. reading, meditation
	All Types	expression of type through appropriate activity that increases self-esteem
Educational (information, self-knowledge, discoveries about the world)	N	perpetual learners of something new through books, independent study, school, etc.
	S	learn about the world through travel, interest groups, etc.
	F	participate in self-discovery or growth workshops
	T	acquire technical knowledge, e.g., computer skills
Social (relationships with others)	F	affiliation, personal interactions
	E	high level of activity with others
Relaxational (stress relief)	All Types	compensation and balance for all types; activity varies with type and lifestyle
Physiological (fitness, health, etc.)	S	more naturally tuned to body
	N	less body awareness, develops later
Aesthetic (pleasure of beauty and good design)	F	harmony in nature, design, and the arts (especially INFP, ISFP); sense of beauty found in order (especially ISTJ, ISFJ)
	N	ingenious pattern of ideas, films, arts, books
	T	elegant logic, e.g., a math or chess problem

or values and instead remain sensitive to the varying needs and values of all types. We can, however, help friends or family members evaluate the quality of their leisure. If their leisure looks unsatisfying or like work, we can ask them how they experience their activity. They may need to experiment with a different approach or attitude—the INTJ tennis player may benefit from approaching an activity without the intention of mastering and controlling it. Listening to music or flying a kite might provide this different kind of play experience.

Personality is a great influence on our attitudes toward play in general. The most obvious influence is the Judgment–Perception preference. An exercise called "Work versus Play" demonstrates this clearly. In this exercise, people are asked to position themselves along an imaginary line or continuum. One end stands for the attitude, "Work and play are interchangeable." The other end stands for the attitude, "I can't play until my work is finished." Invariably, the majority of Perceptive types (P's) chooses the former end, while the majority of Judgment types (J's) chooses the latter. Because J's generally adhere more assiduously to a plan and need to get things done before starting anything new, they tend to view play as something optional or extra, to be done only after all work is completed and loose ends are tied up. This attitude seems particularly true for SJ's, who are not likely to interrupt a work project to play spontaneously.

The Perceiving types, on the other hand, are naturally more flexible; sticking to a schedule is not as important to them as it is to Judging types. They are, therefore, naturally more willing to drop things if a play opportunity arises or if they feel a need to play at a particular moment. They tend to have a high need for playfulness both in their leisure and in their work. Sometimes this need can be irritating to co-workers if it is not channeled in appropriate ways. Perceiving types are likely to pursue leisure activities that do not require much advance planning and organizing, and sometimes they may miss play opportunities because they haven't planned anything in advance. The Judging types, however, may need to "plan to be spontaneous" by blocking off times when they will be more open to the leisure opportunities of the moment, or schedule their time for play.

Extraversion and Introversion, in combination with the Judging or Perceiving preferences, also influence play attitudes. Extraverted Perceiving types may look for highly active and social forms of play, such as volleyball, parties, and dances. Those with Introverted Perceiving preferences tend to choose activities that are more low-key, informal, and personal, such as an intimate dinner party, going to a movie with a friend, and hiking in the mountains alone or with a friend. Of course, after midlife these patterns can change as individuals explore their lesser preferences. Mature Extraverts may find themselves engaging in more solitary forms of recreation than those they would have chosen 20 years earlier. Mature Judging types may be more willing to drop work to play with a friend or spouse, whereas when younger they may have felt compelled to finish work before playing.

This description shows how personality preferences interact with leisure needs. We can apply this idea to our earlier discussion about changes in leisure interests in midlife or thereafter, due to the drive to explore the lesser preferences. If we look at the last category—satisfaction of aesthetic needs, for example—we can see that a dominant Extraverted Thinking type (ESTJ, ENTJ) might become more interested in art and other aesthetic pursuits in later life as part of the exploration of the least preferred Feeling function. So focus will shift from one of these leisure categories to another as we explore our inferior functions.

In sum, the Extraversion–Introversion and Judging–Perceiving preferences probably have more effect on basic attitudes towards play than do the mental functions—Sensing, Intuition, Thinking, and Feeling; these mental functions seem to have more influence on interests and the motivation for leisure. Following are brief sketches of how the sixteen types tend to approach play.

Leisure Styles of the Sixteen Types

ISTJ

Serious and often solitary in their leisure, they apply their concentration and thoroughness to leisure activities. They prefer activities with purpose and concrete outcomes or measurably increased skill. They're deliberate in their approach to play and tend to be little given to spontaneity. Examples of play activities for ISTJ's include: chess, Trivial Pursuit, computer games, aerobics, or golf.

ISFJ

Devoted to significant others in their leisure, they may be the cheering section for another's sport; they are loyal to close friends or relatives in their use of their own leisure time. Low-key yet purposeful, preferring to plan their activities, they often focus on their physical surroundings or on creature comforts. Other examples of ISFJ activities include: special dinners, picnics, nature walks, or watching TV or movies with someone they care for.

ISTP

Characterized by their detached curiosity in leisure activity, whether spelunking or skydiving, they tend to choose activities that are solitary or enjoyed with a risk-taking friend. They often like manipulating mechanical things (planes, jet skis, rifles, etc.). They frequently bring droll humor into play and may seem to shift easily into play activities without drawing attention to themselves or without visible effort to plan. Other examples are: archery, amateur stand-up comedy or stage magic, scuba diving, or rappelling.

ISFP

Quiet, friendly socializing with intimate friends or "hanging out" in a relaxed situation is important. They tend to focus on harmony in relationships and in their environment; thus art, nature, and informal hospitality are good choices for their play activity. They are very easygoing about leisure unless their sense of harmony is disrupted. Physical, aesthetic activities—like dancing and skiing—may appeal to them. Other possibilities are: swimming or relaxing by the pool, learning crafts, or giving or attending small parties.

ESTP

They tend to be highly active and to need stimulation, perhaps through mechanical things or competitive team sports. Activity and competition are often more important than personal relationships in their leisure. They may pick up leisure, physical, or mechanical skills quickly, though they tend to be impatient with reflective sorts of leisure. Other examples include: race car driving, flying, softball, volleyball, or boxing.

ESFP

Outgoing, easygoing, and highly social, they like big parties and gatherings; they're often high-spirited, warm, and friendly in groups. They also tend to interact with others easily through team sports and are quick to join a group that looks like fun. They may enjoy home projects, such as building a deck for parties or putting up preserves for friends. Other recreational possibilities for them are: noncompetitive games, dancing, or basketball.

ESTJ

Since these individuals tend to be practical realists, they often choose activities with productive outcomes, such as tinkering at home or building a greenhouse. They may enjoy taking the initiative to organize and run things, so community organizations or volunteer activities are good leisure possibilities for them. Their interest in nature tends toward identifying and categorizing natural phenomena; they are less interested in physical activity for its own sake than are some other types. They may enjoy taking up a structured sport, such as golf, especially if they can combine it with work-related social activities.

ESFJ

Warm-hearted and communicative, they tend to be popular and active in committees, church and volunteer activities, and other group efforts. They may enjoy celebrating holidays, family traditions, and gathering of friends, perhaps by planning and executing special occasions; they are often considered thoughtful of others. ESFJ's tend to enjoy sports that permit socializing. Other good play activities for them include choral music, casual volleyball, cooking classes or parties, and church activities.

INFJ

Their originality is often expressed through reflective, solitary activities such as reading and music (playing, composing, or appreciating it). The quiet warmth characteristic of this type may show in their social preference for small intimate gatherings. Their energy for physical activity may seem low to more exuberant types. Other play activities that appeal to INFJ's include artistic and cultural events, informational reading, and collecting aesthetic objects.

INTJ

With their original minds they often enjoy games of strategy. They like to challenge their intuition through attending films and cultural events or reading. Their independent nature may lead them to individualistic sports such as swimming and backpacking. They tend to be critical of their own performance in leisure activities, since mastery is important to them. Often serious and purposeful in their leisure choices, they might find satisfaction in visiting museums, running marathons, or studying a new subject.

INFP

INFP's tend to be private in their enthusiasms and often enjoy artistic activities such as creative writing, playing music, keeping a journal, or taking photographs. Their love of language may lead them to collect poems, quotes, and books. They generally prefer intimate, informal social encounters and dislike large conventional gatherings. Although they have a strong need for time alone and personal expression in their leisure, they may neglect this because of overcommitment to work. Other recreational possibilities for them include appreciating nature, visiting art museums, or attending films and performances.

INTP

Their tendency to be quiet and reserved is expressed in their preference for solitary leisure choices; they may not enjoy parties or conventional kinds of socializing and sports. They often enjoy activities with an intellectual focus—reading, cultural events, or chess. Although solitary leisure is essential to them because of their reflective nature, it may often be neglected, because their intuition draws them into many work activities—which they then feel must be completed competently. Other options for them might include backpacking, hiking, or meditation.

ENFP

ENFP's tend to be warmly enthusiastic about many kinds of leisure, including imaginative play possibilities beyond the conventional or obvious. They are often active and people-focused in sports and gatherings. They may appreciate art and be amateur performers. They often need lots of stimulation and try to bring elements of play into their work. Leisure options for them might include reading fiction, playing an instrument, acting in civic theater, writing poetry or songs, attending performances and films, or dancing.

ENTP

Often stimulating company, ENTP's like to be around exciting people in unconventional surroundings. Their desire for novelty attracts them to unique events. Their love of adventure leads them to enjoy travel and risk-taking activities. They are easygoing about leisure, often preferring not to plan it. Possibilities include travel to exotic places, exploring new activities, or attending unusual cultural events.

ENFJ

Conviviality is very important to ENFJ's; their concern for others may lead them to enjoy initiating social events and personal gestures. They appreciate literature and the arts and may tend to be less interested in physical activity and competitive sports than many of the other types. They often approach leisure with plans and structure and may feel responsible for others' leisure. Play possibilities for them include reading, visiting museums, collecting and telling stories, or gourmet cooking.

ENTJ

ENTJ's may be hearty, outgoing leaders in many activities, organizing a group of friends or their community. Play is usually possible for them only after they feel that their work is finished. They usually enjoy parties and competitive sports. Other options are: attending sporting events, racing sailboats, or planning social events in which they can mix business with pleasure, such as golf with clients or associates.

Having looked at various play activities to discover how they satisfy adult needs and express personality, we will now give some attention to work itself. The next chapter asks how we can find play in our work.

Think About ...

1. Which of the six categories of leisure needs are most important to you? (See pp. 39 and 40.) Rank all six from most to least important and give examples of each in your life.

    1)

    2)

    3)

    4)

    5)

    6)

2. Has the ranking of these six categories changed for you over the years? If so, how?

3. How do you think your personality type affects your leisure needs in these six categories?

4. If you prefer Judging, how flexible are you able to be in your play? Do you plan times to be spontaneous? Can you take a break from work to play, or is play relegated to leftover time and energy—if there is any?

5. If you prefer Perceiving, are you able to organize and plan for leisure activities important to you? Do you find conflicts in your work and personal environments in regard to spontaneity and playfulness versus planfulness and seriousness? How can you manage these potential conflicts?

6. How might your preference for Extraversion or Introversion influence your energy level and leisure activities?

Chapter 5

Finding Play at Work

Individual needs are satisfied through work, from basic survival needs to those of self-actualization and type development. Work may bring some of the same kinds of satisfactions as those brought by the aesthetic, educational, psychological, social, relaxational, and physiological categories associated with leisure. The first four categories can be more easily satisfied through work than can relaxational or physiological needs. For example, the aesthetic need can be fulfilled in architecture and design, the educational in training and professional development, the psychological by completing tasks that increase self-esteem and provide intellectual challenge, and the social through positive interactions on the job.

While most people clearly differentiate their work from their play, others report blurred distinctions between the two. For some individuals, work and play are synonymous—they conceive of play as a state of mind or attitude that they also find at work. It lends an experience of freedom, of flowing with the work activity, and of complete absorption. It seems that this playlike quality is more likely to occur when the dominant or preferred function is used on the job; it rarely happens when people must use their least preferred functions. Since the dominant function is the one we have developed and trust the most, we are much more likely to gain the satisfaction of work well done when using it.

The following paragraphs give examples of kinds of work activities that might be most satisfying for each of the four dominant functions. The assumption is that we have more chance to play at work when engaged in activities that express our dominant function.

Sensing

People with introverted Sensing dominant (ISFJ and ISTJ) might particularly enjoy activities that involve gathering discrete elements of information or material and organizing them into some kind of structure or system. For example, an ISTJ architect may find play in the gathering of specifications and client requirements for a building, carefully contemplating these pieces of information, and finally ordering them into a design solution. An ISFJ elementary school teacher may derive great pleasure from searching out, examining, acquiring, and planning the use of instructional materials for the coming school year.

Individuals who favor extraverted Sensing (ESTP and ESFP) enjoy a high level of action and interaction with others; they tend to enjoy activities that require common sense, attention to realities, and an understanding of things or conditions knowable through the five senses. An ESTP may find play in work as a sales representative—traveling, meeting clients, attending to orders, noticing where a new or better sale could be made, and having a flexible work schedule. An ESFP may merge work and play through coaching and work in recreational therapy.

Intuition

People with dominant introverted Intuition (INTJ and INFJ) find satisfaction in contemplating ideas or possibilities and using their imagination in reflection. They can become absorbed in their own inner world and in the creative process as designers, writers, researchers, and so on. An INTJ behavioral science researcher may enjoy asking questions about human behavior, spectating on possible hypotheses, designing a research methodology, and gathering data or observations so as to see the patterns. An INFJ interior designer specializing in large commercial interiors may play with internal visual possibilities and creative solutions, and in effect invent self-contained worlds or environments.

People with extraverted Intuition (ENTP and ENFP) gain great pleasure from using their imagination and creative problem solving in the world around them. They like brainstorming and generating possibilities through interaction with others. They are happiest when they can take a new idea and explore its possibilities—as opposed to individuals with introverted Intuition, who thoughtfully shape the idea internally and examine it from all angles before showing it to the world. An ENTP may find play in starting new businesses—getting an idea for a new product or service, devising the business plan and image, getting started, and then selling it to others interested in the day-to-day operation. An ENFP may find playful absurdity and abandonment in college teaching, which may be viewed as something akin to performance.

Thinking

Those with dominant introverted Thinking (ISTP and INTP) find pleasure in thoughtful analysis of data, things, or systems, and in placing those data in logical order (ISTP) or solving a complex problem with logic (INTP). An ISTP may become absorbed in taking apart a machine, clock, or instrument that is not working, figuring out the problem, and resolving it in an efficient, resourceful way. An INTP may become fascinated by a complex computer programming problem and derive much satisfaction from analyzing it and creating an efficient, conceptually elegant solution.

Individuals with extraverted Thinking preferences (ESTJ and ENTJ) get the most satisfaction from making action-oriented judgments using logic. An ESTJ forensic anthropologist may play detective, gathering evidence from the scene of a crime and coming to logical conclusions. An ENTJ manager in a large corporation may find that creating new organizational structures and systems is as much fun as playing board games of strategy.

Feeling

People whose dominant preference is introverted Feeling (ISFP and INFP) find satisfaction in work that offers an opportunity for personal expression and brings personal meaning to deeply held values. For example, an ISFP physical education teacher to the handicapped may gain intense satisfaction from teaching students to ski or swim. An INFP who is a writer may find writing to be an absorbing, playful kind of experience.

Those with extraverted Feeling (ESFJ and ENFJ) derive particular satisfaction from directing their feeling values and people skills through outward action. They find satisfaction in leading a group, helping others, or exercising their social skills. An ESFJ dental hygienist may enjoy the part of the job that requires making people feel at ease by finding out about them and making conversation. An ENFJ with many jobs— minister, trainer, and so on—may most enjoy a role as professional toastmaster, a role that requires good humor and warmth to create a convivial atmosphere. Work becomes play under such circumstances.

The Flow Experience at Work

These examples show how exercising one's dominant function can lead to satisfaction, pleasure, and even a playful feeling on the job. Some may even experience Csikszentmihalyi's "flow experience" described earlier. The flow experience was discussed in relation to leisure, but it can be considered in relation to work as well. The flow experience at work occurs most often when people use their dominant function, without interruption from activities requiring use of the lesser functions. For example, Csikszentmihalyi studied surgeons, many of whom have Sensing and Thinking preferences. These surgeons reported the flow experience in their work as they performed the detailed and precise activities of surgery (S) and practiced the objective, decisive approach (T) it required. Remember that this is in contrast to how the flow experience can be felt in play, which often derives from use of the *least* preferred function where there is less of the pressure regarding performance or outcome that is usually associated with work. As pointed out earlier, it is difficult to use the less preferred functions comfortably when anxious or under stress.

The same general conditions must be met in work as in leisure to experience flow. Attention must be extremely focused—in a kind of "tunnel vision," as one Wimbledon tennis champion termed it. This focus reduces the field of attention by selecting out all but the essentials. There must also be a period of time without interruption or distraction. Attention can be further focused by attending to very specific elements of the target event, such as the flight of a tennis ball or the contact point of a surgeon's scalpel. The event must be challenging enough so as to be able to become absorbed in it, yet not so difficult as to unduly stress the individual's capabilities. Matching challenge with ability supports the observation that flow is more likely when the dominant function is being used to do the work.

When a group of adults with different personality types and occupations were asked whether they ever experienced play or flow in their work, they reported as shown in the list below. Their responses were characteristic of their psychological types and more specifically of their favorite preferences.

- An INFP English professor reported flow experiences in teaching. He spent five or ten minutes preparing for class and then upon facing the students would count on a kind of unconscious self to take over, as if in a magical way. He drew from a Feeling state in himself and from the group, and from Intuition in finding creative possibilities within the teaching situation.

- An ENFP therapist and consultant reported flow experiences in both work roles. Sometimes when doing individual psychotherapy or making presentations to groups, he described feeling as if the words and actions were coming without conscious effort. He considered this his best and most inspired work; like the English professor, he was drawing upon Intuition and Feeling.

- An INTP planner said he rarely experienced flow because of the many interruptions at his office. The few times he did become absorbed, losing track of time and self, were when he had long blocks of uninterrupted time with which to solve problems on his computer.

- An ENFJ high school composition instructor frequently achieved a flow experience while planning lessons, though not while actually teaching. Planning engaged her intuition, feeling, and judgment in a way that she found totally absorbing.

- An INTJ anthropology professor reported a flow experience occasionally when reading books in preparation for courses. She described becoming unaware of turning the pages, identifying completely with the author's rhythm and viewpoint, even altering her breathing to this rhythm. The writer's style, her own ability to concentrate, and a lack of interruptions were the key factors for her.

- An ISTJ who was initially uncomfortable with the idea of "losing herself" during flow later cited several work experiences in which she lost track of time and became absorbed. These experiences included serious academic writing and computer programming.

- An ISFJ nurse experienced flow when teaching natural childbirth classes to receptive, interested participants who gave her their full attention. She was then able to provide information in her preferred, step-by-step, organized way. During the flow experience, she told jokes without effort and communicated a great deal of information in a good-humored way.

- An ESFP professional working with residential college students rarely experienced flow at work, except during times of high activity and excitement—as in rush week, when he worked 80 or 90 hours running from one activity to the next. An important condition was the feeling of leadership and control and the energy he derived from being around people.

- An ESTP college student personnel professional reported the flow experience during orientation and staff training. Flow, for her, came from going from group to group and doing many things at once. She enjoyed juggling activities and shifting gears from one thing to another, all done effortlessly.

This small sample demonstrates how all individuals can have pleasant, energizing flow experiences at work very much like their most positive leisure or play experiences. They felt they were performing at a higher level than usual without any particular effort. As in play, they derived intrinsic value from performing their work for its own sake—not for the usual extrinsic rewards normally associated with it.

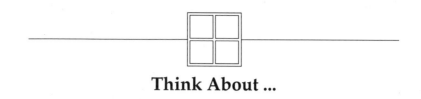

Think About ...

Note: If you are not employed outside your home, consider homemaking, studying, or maintenance activities your work when answering the following questions.

1. How is work an expression of your dominant function?

2. Is there a large portion of your work that demands use of your less preferred functions? If so, how does this affect you?

3. Are there ways in which you could change your work to make better use of your strengths and preferences—in your work environment, tasks, work sequences, structuring of duties, and so forth?

4. Do you ever experience flow in your work? Describe when and under what conditions this happens.

5. What can you do to increase flow opportunities at work?

6. Which of the six categories of needs satisfaction occur in your work—psychological, educational, social, aesthetic, relaxational and physiological?

Chapter 6

Balancing
Work and Play

What is balance, and how can you know when you have it? Often it's hard to tell whether someone's lifestyle is balanced or not—we'd have to inquire about that person's feelings and attitudes toward his or her lifestyle, and about his or her physical and mental health. Balance can be thought of as the particular combination of work and play that meets an individual's needs. The proportions of work and play will be influenced by variables such as personality type, age, gender, health, socioeconomic situation, and developmental stage.

Balance

When people do not have balance in their lives, they often feel stress to the point of *distress* and burnout. Signs include loss of sense of humor, loss of sexual interest, loss of appetite, general malaise, irritability, physical reactions such as headaches and lower back pain, difficulty getting up in the morning even after a good night's sleep, or a perception that everything looks "grey." Although other factors can cause these symptoms besides burnout, it is useful to evaluate one's lifestyle to see if there is a healthy balance of work and play.

Many people in the helping professions burn out because they give tirelessly to others, come home to give again to their families and friends, do not assertively claim time for themselves, and finally feel utterly depleted. Many of these professionals are Feeling types who often have more difficulty than Thinking types in asserting their needs. The S's and J's can burn out by taking their responsibilities too seriously and not letting up until all work is done, leaving no time for themselves. ENP's can burn out from taking on too many projects and not using auxiliary judgment (T or F) to prioritize projects and exclude some that are more tantalizing yet less important. They then become overloaded, despite their strong interest in play. Each type has its own traps that can lead to burnout.

The converse is also possible. An individual could be out of balance because of too much play and not enough meaningful work. A stereotype of this imbalance is the "eternal boy" who jets around from one party or adventure to the next but feels empty of achievement or self-esteem. People who are unemployed for any length of time often feel out of balance, too. Retirees, for example, may experience personal loss when they stop working. Work gives us a sense of accomplishment, identity, purpose, and worth. We meet many of our psychological and social needs, as well as material needs, through work; we want to feel that we mean something in the world and that we're of use.

Scripts or Archetypes

Another way to think about lifestyle and balance is by looking at life *scripts* as reflected through *archetypes*, a term associated with Jung and interpreted as broad patterns of behavior or life themes, often represented symbolically in our culture through fairy tales, art, or mythology. For example, the *Cinderella archetype* represents the theme of working hard, graciously bearing sorrow, and being so long-suffering that finally someone recognizes her goodness and rewards her. This archetype could be translated into a work-play lifestyle that emphasizes hard work without immediate reward but with the expectation of eventual recognition and reward: Someday in the future there will be love, leisure, luxury, and happiness. The Guzies, who have conducted archetype research, identify several male and female archetypes that we commonly live by, through which we often find identity and fulfillment, and which may shape our attitudes toward work and play. The *Mother archetype* finds identity and fulfillment in cherishing, nurturing, and protecting. If she carries this theme too far, she may smother her family or become a martyr by only being able to give comfort to others while denying her own needs. The male equivalent is the *Father archetype*, for which the same dynamics apply. Individuals living out these archetypes are less likely to deliberately incorporate the play they need into their lives because their sense of obligation and duty takes precedent.

The opposite archetypes to Mother/Father are the *Companion* and *Eternal Boy/Girl archetypes*. The Companion finds fulfillment through offering intellectual, spiritual, and sexual companionship in personal relationships. The so-called Eternal Boy similarly looks for fulfillment, though in a more self-focused and restless perpetual quest; he goes his own way and does not concern himself with permanence. Peter Pan is a good example from literature. These individuals have a high need for play; they relate to others through play and may be more likely to create play at work.

These are a few examples of how archetypes or life themes may further shape personality type and our needs for balance in work and play. We should ask ourselves whether we carry with us some life script that instructs us to lead our lives in a particular way. Are there certain beliefs or assumptions about living that shape our overall choices in work and play? One script example is that of the ant and the grasshopper: The ant believes that one should work diligently to accumulate assets for a secure future, whereas the grasshopper believes one should enjoy the moment and let the future take care of itself. The ant stresses work and postpones play—perhaps indefinitely; the grasshopper plays rather than works.

Another script is one often found among adult children of alcoholics who feel that to be worthy and loved they must try to please everyone, including their boss, family, friends, and clients. They think that by doing more than is expected they will be accepted and loved. A script like this prevents an individual from being assertive enough to make sure that personal needs are met through a balance between work and play. In fact, such people frequently are unable to identify their own needs because they are so focused on those of others. They may be overachievers at work, they may have difficulty playing and being spontaneous, and their work and work relationships may suffer from an extreme and rigid approach.

Life scripts should be periodically reevaluated to see whether they truly fit our needs at a given point in our lives. We must question if we truly embrace a particular life script for ourselves, or whether we have accepted the script without examination. Are we living out a script someone else has imposed on us, or one we have chosen freely?

Rhythms of Work and Play

Balance for many involves daily inclusion of meaningful and satisfying work and play. For others, play is reserved for weekends. The latter lifestyle puts a burden on the weekend to balance a week's work. Often people place such unrealistic expectations on their weekends that they end up disappointed. People return to work irritable on Mondays because they felt their weekends were too short-lived. Most people would benefit from building in some form of leisure daily or every other day. Small amounts of daily leisure time can be effective, such as taking a hot bubble bath after dinner or jogging for 15 minutes immediately after working all day in a sedentary job. Daily balance necessitates a *conscious*, purposeful approach to living and taking charge of one's life, instead of merely reacting to life's demands.

Some people relegate play and leisure to vacations. If vacation consists of only one or two weeks a year, there is certainly going to be little balance between work and play. Of 10,369 Americans who responded to a survey about vacation attitudes and behaviors, the overwhelming majority saw vacation as an "essential escape valve" but reported a gap between vacation fantasy and reality. This study, conducted by Rubenstein for *Psychology Today*,[8] reported a tug-of-war between work and leisure values as respondents expressed a desire for more leisure time for personal growth; few reported a desire for more time to advance their careers. The most frequent reasons given for taking vacations were:

- rest and relaxation (63%)

- escape routine (52%)

- visit friends or relatives (45%)

- recharge, get renewed (45%)

- explore new places (35%)

Thirteen percent of the sample were classified as workaholics because they reported working more than 65 hours per week. Of this group, 42 percent reported taking *less* vacation time than they were due, although they reported similar levels of satisfaction with their lives as the nonworkaholics. The workaholics reported that on vacation they felt "more harassed and tired"; they also took longer to relax when on vacation. The prototype is the driven, energetic executive who is constantly on the go at work and fits swimming, squash, or running into his or her tight schedule. For workaholics, too much leisure can be stressful. These individuals must determine through self-examination whether their balance of leisure and work is appropriate for them.

This study also revealed that the respondents who enjoyed their vacations the most tended to relish excitement and adventure, to enjoy meeting people, and to not be overly concerned about such matters as comfort and convenience. They were reported to be more energetic than most and not particularly cautious. This same group did not see vacations as more important than work. "Most readers said they would continue to work even if they could live comfortably without doing so. They do not seek a leisure-filled life, but a better *balance* of time between work, personal growth, and family."[9] This study supports the concept of balance between work and leisure, as well as the notion that there can be no single formula to describe balance in work and play for everyone.

Real People and Balance

Perhaps it is helpful to give several examples of how real people of different types have achieved their own kind of balance between work and play. Tom is an ENTP field biologist who works for a large organization but has a great deal of creative autonomy. He has very few developed leisure interests and does not play any sports or engage in any regular physical activity. He is reactive to others in his leisure—if his wife, children, or friends suggest doing something, he is responsive and spontaneously playful. Unless someone else plans an activity, though, his leisure comprises unplanned, low-key activities such as reading in a wide range of subjects, listening to music, and watching television. Most of Tom's play occurs through his work: collecting specimens in the field, studying them, exploring new places, traveling, and so forth. He works long hours, but he doesn't perceive this as work. His job allows full expression of his preferences for Intuition and Thinking, and his lifestyle suits an Extraverted Perceiver's need for freedom, adventure, and action.

Elliot, on the other hand, is an INFP who is fairly bored and unchallenged by much of his daily work routine. He provides technical services in a university setting. He derives some satisfaction from helping others and working with them to solve technical problems, but has long ago mastered all the challenges of the job. There are no real surprises left in the job for him, and only rarely are there opportunities for major creative changes. Elliot has decided to remain in this position for the time being because of the security and the needs of his spouse. He does not have children. To bring balance, he has carefully and consciously shaped his leisure time. Since he deals with many people all day long, his leisure is usually of a solitary nature or involves one other person. He has always played the guitar and been an avid reader of fiction. At midlife he has added an intense interest in woodworking, exploring his Sensing and Thinking functions through wood and technical equipment. He leaves work as promptly as he can and absorbs himself in his newly created woodworking shop. His leisure is compensatory and developmental. He attends to his physiological needs through walking the long distance to work several times a week. Elliot also enjoys hiking in the mountains by himself or with one companion who will respect and appreciate nature in silence.

Jill, an ENFP psychotherapist, realized in her mid-thirties when her children were in elementary school that her life was imbalanced. As a professional, wife, and mother, her time was absorbed by duties and responsibilities; she had not been very assertive about pursuing some of her own leisure interests. Her work was sedentary, so she felt a need for highly active physical leisure but found it difficult to schedule this. After self-exploration and discussion with her family, she began consciously to make time for herself to play tennis, volleyball, and swim. This meant letting go of some archetypal "super-mom" behaviors; it also required a change in both her attitude and that of her family. She was able to use early mornings and lunch hours for leisure activities such as exercising or socializing with friends. Jill also incorporated many elements of play into her work—sharing humor with clients, acting in spontaneous and novel ways, and combining some professional contacts with play activities. Her life became much more satisfying once she had given herself permission to include more playfulness and leisure activity into her life.

Challenges to Balance

Homemakers with young children, especially those with additional jobs outside the home, often have the greatest difficulty in creating leisure or play for themselves. Tony, an ISTJ, became fairly successful at achieving balance through assertively organizing her days and negotiating shared childcare and household chores with her husband. Her children were both of preschool age. She took her homemaking duties very seriously, as do most STJ's, and was conscientious about completing these to near perfection. Tony worked out childcare with her husband, sitters, and friends so that she could swim daily and do aerobics several times a week. Relaxational and physiological leisure satisfaction were high priorities for her at that time in her life. She discovered that it was difficult for her to relax and play with the children in the house after she had cleaned it, but could be spontaneous and playful if she took them to a park. In this outdoor setting, she could enjoy playing with her children because she avoided getting caught up in keeping her house perfectly neat.

Balance is also a challenge for people in dual-career marriages, especially where there are dependent children or other dependents such as an ill parent being cared for in the home. A National Institute of Mental Health Study found that 80 to 90 percent of housework was still done by women and that these women had very little leisure in their lives: "For some, five minutes alone in the shower was the height of the day for leisure." In many dual-career households, women continue their traditional roles as well as working outside the home, leaving no time for leisure. The dual-career lifestyle necessitates a renegotiation of household responsibilities if both women and men are to balance work and play.

Other factors affect balance between work and play. Individuals may have to find creative solutions to limitations or obstacles such as physical handicaps, lack of financial resources, geographical location and transportation, time constraints, lack of skills and knowledge, and family and household responsibilities. Personal relationships can be either obstacles or incentives to balance. If someone is caring for a sick parent at home besides working full time, it becomes challenging to include sufficient leisure. Some spouses are threatened by their partners' play activities and may try to limit them. Conflicts can arise between partners about the amount and kind of leisure activities to pursue.

If you conduct an assessment of work and play in your life, you may discover that some changes are desirable. We may succeed in creating a balance for a while, but life circumstances and changes within ourselves may create the need to modify our work and play over time. Adjustment in every lifestyle is called for periodically. How do we bring about change in our lives? What are some strategies to bring about the balance we desire? How can we help our family and friends achieve the necessary changes? The following chapters address these issues in some detail.

Think About ...

1. Do you ever feel overly stressed or burned out? If so,

    a) What are your personal symptoms or signs of burnout?

    b) Under what conditions do you experience burnout?

    c) Would changes in work and play proportions prevent or alleviate burnout? How?

2. Can you recognize patterns, stories, scripts, or archetypes in the way you lead your life? How do they influence your work and play balance?

3. How often do you incorporate play into your life—daily? every other day? weekends? only on vacation? never? Would you like to change this in some way? How?

4. What part do vacations have in your efforts to balance work and play?

5. What is your idea of a satisfying vacation? Which of the six leisure needs are met and what aspects of your personality are expressed?

6. In thinking back over the vacations you have taken, can you identify one that was frustrating or unsatisfying for you? Explain why and speculate on how it could have been more enjoyable.

7. If you could create the ideal balance in your life right now, what would it look and feel like?

8. If you are a parent, how do you balance your needs for leisure with your family responsibilities? Are there things you would like to change?

9. If you are in a dual-career marriage, do you negotiate household responsibilities? What, if anything, would you wish to change?

Chapter 7

Balancing Work and Play
in Relationships

Couples in long-term relationships often have different personality preferences, especially if they chose each other when young. Opposites often are attracted to each other in youth because each has something the other seeks. For example, consider a couple comprising an Extravert and an Introvert. Each brings certain strengths: The Extravert is action-oriented, initiating, and gregarious, while the Introvert offers thoughtful reactions, the ability to listen well, and the capacity to consider the couple's affairs in more depth than the Extravert might. Differences in personality type are a source of complementarity, but they are often also a source of conflict and miscommunication. Individuals with differing preferences bring different interests, values, and attitudes to their life together that have a strong impact on work and play patterns.

Work, Play, and Couples

Enduring couples build relationships upon a wealth of shared experiences, developing bonds through shared joy, pain, pleasure, and successful problem solving. Such couples share the work of running a household and may share professional interests as well. Play is very important in developing and maintaining intimacy because play enriches a couple's shared history, builds common interests, enhances communication, and provides a reserve of good feelings and memories against inevitable rough times. Let's look at how type differences or similarities affect play for couples.

Extraversion–Introversion

When members of a couple differ in their preferences for Extraversion or Introversion, their leisure activities are also likely to differ—especially the amount of socializing they desire and the amount of private time they need. Extraverts, for example, may tend to fill a weekend with one activity after another, while Introverts may prefer a slower pace or fewer obligations. Extraverts are more likely to make time for many activities on vacations; this high activity level can be overwhelming to introverted partners, who tend to prefer fewer activities performed in more depth. Those activities, such as listening to music and reading, may appear too low-key to Extraverts.

Introverts and Extraverts differ in their ideas about the nature of "home." For those with preferences for Introversion, home is often a sanctuary, a place to renew oneself away from the busy pace of the world. Their extraverted partners, on the other hand, may wish to have friends drop in frequently or may prefer the activity and stimulation of going out more often than Introverts do. Introverts tend to find renewal by going inside themselves, especially if their work requires Extraversion. Extraverts tend to be rejuvenated by action and interaction with others. Individuals functioning at work primarily in the opposite mode to their preference have a greater need to express their true preference in their leisure. An extraverted spouse, for example, whose only company during the day is a toddler, may have a strong need for leisure activities that involve other adults.

These differences between Extraversion and Introversion are valuable for balance in couples' lives. Extraverted partners often contribute energy and initiative to the couple's leisure, while introverted partners bring balance through their appreciation for depth within interests and time spent alone (for both the individuals and the couple).

Couples differing in their preference for Extraversion and Introversion need to be sensitive to each other's needs and to find ways to share experiences while making sure their own needs are met. Extraverts should not, for example, assume that their introverted partners are eager for more house guests. Extraverts might occasionally go out without their partners to meet their higher need for activity and to give their partners some time alone. Introverts, in turn, can pace themselves in order to be more active or excited about some activity that is important to their extraverted partners. Partners need to respect the differing rhythms of opposite preferences and find ways to allow expression of those differences without construing disagreements about leisure rhythms as deliberate conflict or power struggles.

Partners may more easily understand each other's needs when they share the same preference. However, there can be problems here as well. Two Extraverts may find themselves so involved with activities that they spend little time focused on each other, rarely taking time to listen to what the other is saying. They may have such busy lives that little leisure time is left for the relationship. Two Extraverts may need to slow down and listen to each other by taking a quiet walk, going out for coffee, giving each other a massage, and so forth. Couples whose partners are also introverted sometimes report that "nothing much happens" in their leisure; neither may be inclined to initiate leisure activities and social events. To find some balance in their leisure, they may want to call upon extraverted friends. One couple, an INTJ and ISTP, have several very extraverted friends they "import" when they want more stimulation. Another couple, an ISFJ and INFP, decided to experiment with throwing a large party and called upon their extraverted friend to show them how to plan it. Most of the time, couples preferring Introversion have the comfort of the same pace and flow in their activities and social lives.

Sensing–Intuition

Differences in how information is perceived can provide useful balance in leisure for couples. The Intuitive partner may come up with a new idea for shared play; the Sensing partner can then provide practical approaches that make the idea happen. For example, the Intuitive partner may suggest a vacation to some exotic place. The Sensing partner may enjoy researching the location and planning such details as airline flights, hotel reservations, transportation, and tours. In this way each partner contributes something to the leisure experience. A satisfying vacation for both emerges in which there is a balance between structure and discovery, between manipulation of information and encounters with novelty. Vacation planning for these kinds of couples becomes a form of play that satisfies both the Sensing and the Intuitive preferences. One couple, an ENFP and an ESTJ, handles vacations this way: The ENFP chooses a vacation spot for its sense of discovery and adventure; the ESTJ studies maps, plans destinations, and arranges travel, hotels, transportation, and tours.

Partners must understand the differences in ways of perceiving in order to tolerate and respect certain behaviors. For example, on a nature walk, a couple differing in Sensing and Intuition might become frustrated because the Sensing partner wants to be able to name every plant and bird while the Intuitive partner prefers to focus on the overall panorama, the intangibles in the experience of nature. One is looking at the forest, and the other is looking carefully at each tree. Each partner needs to approach nature, or any other leisure activity, from his or her own perspective. The activity can be shared, but the process each uses will be different. Depending on the level of mutual respect and understanding, this process can be either frustrating or fascinating.

When both members of a couple have the same perception preference, communication is easier and approaches to leisure are similar, but complementarity is missing. This may mean that novelty and imagination are absent from the play of two Sensing types, or that attention to practical details and comforts are overlooked by two Intuitive types. For example, such a couple may rarely travel for pleasure because both partners enjoy thinking of places to go but neither likes dealing with the practical aspects of planning a trip.

Thinking–Feeling

Differences in preference on this scale affect values, priorities, and decisions about leisure. Generally, partners with a Feeling preference may place a higher priority on activities that involve others or build relationships. Thinking types may tend to put priority on activities that are focused on development of skills or knowledge. Of course, with continued type development and maturity, partners may change their patterns of work and play as they explore their lesser preferences. These differing priorities can lead to few shared leisure activities or even to conflicts. For example, the Thinking partner of a couple might upset the Feeling partner by indicating to guests at a dinner party that it is late and time for guests to go home. The Feeling individual, though secretly agreeing that it is getting late, is distressed at the bluntness of the other's approach. After guests leave, an argument ensues. The Thinking type is bewildered because the Feeling partner is so upset over what appears to be a harmless, obviously logical comment. The Feeling partner, however, is concerned that friends won't feel welcome in their home. The Thinking partner may observe that the other "always makes a big deal of little inconsequential things," making it difficult for the Thinking type to enjoy these social gatherings. This is a small example, but such disputes can build on each other until there are complex tensions in the way this couple socializes with others. Understanding the consequences of differences in the judgment preference and working to respect each other's styles can reduce this kind of tension.

A couple sharing the Thinking preference may find their social needs unsatisfied in their leisure, especially if both prefer Introversion and Thinking. They may rely more on each other's company and understanding and may feel uneasy about bringing people together or functioning as a couple in social situations. Types whose preferences are similar will have the comfort of their similarity but may sometimes miss the balance of their opposite. For example, two Feeling types may be so concerned with harmony that neither expresses true feelings and goals about how to spend their leisure time. Each is trying to accommodate the other at the expense of not fully developing themselves.

Judgment–Perception

Differences on this scale most often appear as disagreements about the balance of work and play in the couple's life. Judging types, who prefer planning and structure, usually want to complete work before playing. Perceiving types are less concerned about closure, especially in their work; they need more flexibility and spontaneity. Thus, a Perceiving type may spontaneously say, "Hey, let's go for a walk—it's a lovely evening!" The Judging partner responds, "Not right now; I'm trying to finish up this project...maybe later if I get finished." The Perceiving type may interpret such a response this way: He or she doesn't care about our relationship, isn't any fun, isn't interested in doing things with me, and so forth. Eventually, these misinterpretations can lead to open argument, and the Judging partner may feel like the Perceiving partner is making unreasonable demands. Both will feel frustrated. The Perceiving partner must learn to give the Judging type some advance warning and to respect the Judging type's need for completion and planning. The Judging partner needs to learn to let go of plans periodically, perhaps by allowing some time each week for spontaneous activity ("planned spontaneity"). If each can respect the other and develop some appreciation for the partner's preference, frustration will diminish and satisfaction increase. Both can then pride themselves on being adaptable within the relationship.

This conflict (between Judging and Perceiving) can become more intense on vacations or long weekends, when the Judging partner wants to plan out all the available time while the Perceiver wants to leave things open to see what the day will bring. These attitudes can lead to a power struggle unless each acknowledges the other's needs and compromises, allowing some of the time to be planned and some to be open-ended. Each can learn to live with a moderate amount of structure, while remaining willing to let go of plans if something more exciting or interesting comes along. A difference on this preference can be a wonderful balance when it comes to planning vacations. The Judging partner may really enjoy planning the vacation and scheduling reservations, and the Perceiving partner will make sure that spontaneity and surprise are present in their shared leisure.

The Sixteen Types

Remember that the four preference scales combine to make sixteen types, which means a great deal of variability among couples. Differences are usually not due simply to one preference scale; for example, ESTJ's and ISTJ's tend to have a stronger work ethic than INFP's and ENFP's, who may value play highly, especially when developing relationships. Couples with these differences may struggle over such lifestyle issues as work and play—that is, time spent together being playful versus time spent getting work and projects done. Two ESTJ's might experience tension because there is little natural drive toward spontaneity and playfulness. Two

ENFP's might experience tension from the buildup of tasks left incomplete due to their preference for playfulness and spontaneity; neither wants to do certain tasks, and each waits for the other to take the initiative.

Here are some examples that illustrate the conflicts that can arise in the leisure choices of couples with differing preferences:

- An ENTJ insists on social activities with business associates that will further her career. Her ENFP partner objects; he wants social leisure to be "authentic and personal" with close friends.

- An ISFJ woman likes quiet, homey evenings with her ENTP partner and dislikes many of his leisure interests, which involve physical activity and high risk (scuba diving, flying). He is frustrated that their evenings home are not exciting enough.

- An INFP has a strong need to play, but his ISTJ wife gets upset if all the projects on her list are not done first.

- An ESFJ man cannot understand why his INFP partner wants time alone to read, write, or go for solitary walks. He pressures her to spend more time with him and wonders if she really cares as much about him as he does her.

Partners who understand each other's type can accept and respect each other's needs, values, and attitudes. This understanding can eliminate the belief that the partner is being stubborn or difficult. Both have the right to express their type in the relationship. After all, they are in a relationship because they want to share life with each other; this can motivate them to learn to compromise and occasionally practice the other's preference or orientation. This is also a way of developing one's own lesser functions. In relationships that endure over time, partners can help each other to develop the less strong areas of their characters and can appreciate and enjoy these new aspects of their partner.

Type, gender, archetypal scripts, and other factors may all contribute to role specialization within couples. For example, one partner may become the "social director," while the other becomes a passive participant. One may take on the role of initiator, while the other prefers the role of responder or resister. A certain amount of specialization is natural to any couple's existence. Just as in type development we specialize in our dominant function early in life, so do we tend to specialize in our work and play roles within a relationship. In fact, our types may well shape the roles we play in relationships. Just as in type development, however, in later life we may become dissatisfied with being specialists and want to develop previously unexpressed aspects of ourselves—lesser preferences—and try out new roles. Therefore, couples should be sensitive to whether the same partner is always expected to play a certain role, or whether there is enough flexibility within the relationship for both partners to try out new roles and behavior. This means that the partner who is usually not the initiator should be encouraged to follow through with a tentatively expressed interest in organizing a social gathering. Subtle issues of control can underlie these roles. Certain types may prefer to keep control, but it is important to allow enough flexibility for continued development of each individual within the relationship. These experiments in new leisure activities help each partner to develop personally and to keep the relationship fresh and interesting.

Extremes in orientation toward work or play can create serious conflict in relationships. A "workaholic," for example, spends little or no time on leisure and little time with a partner unless that time is work-related. The lack of shared leisure makes this relationship less satisfactory and less likely to grow than others.

On the other hand, leisure also can be taken to extremes. For example, when jogging became popular, articles appeared about people who had become compulsive runners. They had to run a certain number of miles each day or feel guilty and irritable. Another example is illustrated by the golf widow, which implies a separation and lack of shared leisure with the partner. Leisure activities can become compulsions that interfere with relationships and with other daily functioning. There does not appear to be any one type more prone than others to such compulsive behavior.

Individuals need to evaluate their leisure and work behaviors and discern whether there is enough balance for them as individuals and in their relationships. If the relationship is pushed to one side because of extreme attention to work or to some leisure pursuit, then partners must decide whether the relationship is important enough to change their behaviors. Psychological factors and environmental factors can account also for compulsive behavior. Type, however, can be useful in self-evaluation of needs and in understanding the partner's approaches to work and play. Type can facilitate communication about these issues.

Sex as Play

Sex is an important form of communication and play between partners. Some of the differences among the types are reflected in attitudes toward sex and sexual behavior. For instance, SP types may be more spontaneous than SJ's in their sexual behavior. An SP involved with an SJ might become frustrated if the SJ responded to playful sexual overtures with "Not now; I've got this report to write." Much of sexuality is spontaneous by its very nature, and J's can try to practice flexibility when it comes to sex. From the J's point of view, though, it may be difficult to enjoy sex if preoccupied with finishing an important piece of work. However, a J partner may be able to create a perfect romantic evening through careful planning and anticipation of the partner's desires. Judging types, especially SJ's, may also be more likely to let sex—as well as other aspects of their lives—become routine. Routine can reduce the vitality of sexual playfulness or even create conflict, especially if the partner is an Intuitive type.

Sensing and Intuitive differences shape sexual perceptions. Sensing types are more naturally tuned in to their bodies and thus may be more directly and immediately able to experience pleasure or discomfort through their senses. Intuitives are more likely to focus on a fantasy, or an ideal image. What is stimulating and exciting to an Intuitive may be quite different from what is so for a Sensing individual. A Sensing partner can help the intuitive partner experience sensuality by starting slowly with a massage or other tactile activity. The door to sexual communication for Sensing types is the senses, while for intuitive types it is the imagination. Intuitive partners, especially NP's, tend to have a higher need for novelty in their sexual play than do the Sensing types. Intuitives may complain that their Sensing partners don't show enough imagination in their love making. This complaint may be bewildering for the Sensing partner, who is absorbed in the pleasures of the interaction and doesn't know what imagination has to do with it. Couples who differ on this preference can experiment with these two different ways of perceiving to find ways of maximizing playful sexuality.

Thinking and Feeling differences affect sexual play as well. Feeling types, especially Extraverts, will probably need more explicit appreciations and feedback during sexual play than will Thinking types. Thinking types will need to know that they are competent lovers. NF's have a strong need to talk about the relationship, and this talk can be bewildering and distracting to a partner with Sensing and Thinking preferences. Partners need to be aware of these differences in style so that they are not hurt or misunderstood when naturally expressing their sexual play. Humor is often enriching in sexual play, and the ability to laugh at differences *together* can make the interaction that much more satisfying.

Couples Summary

Just as enduring intimacy does not mean total immersion in each other, so couples' leisure does not mean sharing all the same interests and activities. Each partner needs to find leisure that expresses and develops the self. The benefits of these separate leisure experiences can be brought by each partner into the relationship to enrich it and make it more diverse. Some time must be set aside, however, for shared leisure and play; this takes awareness, communication, and negotiation. Relationships may be evaluated by one partner on the basis of shared activities and sex, and by the other on the basis of shared feelings and intimacies. Such differences in evaluation have strong implications for the nature of play within relationships.

Work, Play, and Families

Play is as valuable to relationships and communication among family members as it is between partners. Personality types, age differences, and other factors influence the nature of a family's work and play patterns. Play is, paradoxically, serious business for children; it is their vehicle for growth and development. Through play they rehearse future behavior, develop skills, and master their environments. When parents play with their children, they support this development. Parents also communicate with their children through play. Expressions of feelings, thoughts, teachings, and so forth are much more effectively conveyed to young children through a play context. By playing with their children, parents can offer a context for parent-child relationships to develop other than that of the parent as provider or disciplinarian. By interacting with children as equals during play, parents can help them develop confidence and self-esteem.

When children see parents play, they see adult models who can still have fun despite their adult responsibilities. Many young people today are afraid to grow up because the adults they see look bored, depressed, or preoccupied by heavy responsibilities. Children don't have to feel guilty about their parents' hard work on their behalf if they also see adults having fun. It is liberating for children to see their parents play. Furthermore, children who see their parents playing *together* have more positive attitudes about adult relationships and marriage. They also come to realize that their parents are individuals, not one-dimensional caretakers.

Play is therapeutic to families and to marriages. Families in trouble often have unsatisfying leisure patterns as well as poor communication. For example, in many families, parents have been uninvolved in the day-to-day raising of children; they work long hours to provide material support for the family. When their children reach adolescence, these parents discover that they are living with strangers. The children have turned into separate individuals, and there is no common ground. Sharing a family culture and a play history as children grow can give families inner resources to draw on when changes occur. Sometimes uninvolved parents can become reconnected with their adolescent strangers through an effort to find leisure activities to share.

Naturally, leisure patterns in families change as families go through various life stages. When children are very young, parents are usually not as free to play and may choose activities that can be done at home or with small children. Sometimes one parent is responsible for all the caretaking, while the other parent has the freedom to play. Dual-career marriages can make it a challenge to balance work and play, especially if there are young children. These couples must consciously examine their priorities and strive to make time for shared family leisure. Families with teenagers have more flexibility in their range of leisure activities and more freedom from caretaking. Teenagers often become pleasant play companions. Grown children and extended families can easily use leisure as a way of maintaining contact with family members and of redefining relationships as family members grow and change.

As older family members move toward retirement, their leisure time increases and takes on greater importance, since this will be their main source of stimulation and need fulfillment. If retiring family members have not developed play interests, conflict may develop in the family. For example, a successful physician who retires expecting to spend most of his time on the golf course may find after a year or so that this activity alone fails to provide enough intellectual stimulation. His spouse will be frustrated by his moping presence in the house, and his grown children will become concerned about the effects of his dissatisfaction upon his physical and mental health and upon their parents' marriage. Positive, flexible leisure patterns and attitudes developed with friends and family over time will make the transition to retirement smoother.

Family members are likely to have differing personality types that influence leisure needs. There may be a prevailing climate or set of attitudes toward work and play set by the predominant type in the family or by a dominant family member that may not be comfortable for other family members with different type preferences. Tension is probably most evident when the Extravert or the Introvert is in the minority. The introverted daughter in a family of Extraverts, for example, may learn to be more extraverted to keep up with the rest of the family, but also must find time alone, perhaps through reading in her room. Car trips or other situations in which she can't physically get away may remain difficult for her. Another example is a midthirties couple planning to have their first child; married for ten years, they both prefer an introverted life. They may be afraid of having an extraverted child who will disrupt their quiet household. If family members learn about type, they can appreciate each other's differences and make needed accommodations. Knowledge of personality preferences gives family members a common language with which to communicate their individual needs. Families can maintain good humor about their personality differences and try to see potential conflicts in an amusing light. The introverted daughter, for instance, can learn to tease her family about all the extraverted activity going on, and the family can learn to hear her need, and maybe their own as well, to slow down the pace a little.

Family vacations can magnify differences in personality type. It is wise to take type preferences into account in planning a vacation together so each member can feel comfortable. Age differences make this even more challenging. Families who don't play together on a daily or weekly basis may find vacations together disappointing because they lack skill in family leisure. Tension may arise from the unfamiliarity of these new leisure relationships.

Just as marriage partners need to have both individual and shared leisure interests, so do children. One way that children move toward individuation—that is, development of their own personalities—is to freely choose some leisure interests of their own. Families that demand too much togetherness don't allow this development process to occur. The goal should be a balance between individual, couple, and family leisure pursuits.

Think About ...

1. What leisure activities do you share with your partner?

2. Do you want to make changes in your shared leisure—for example, increase frequency, try some new activity, decrease time together? If so, what changes would you like to make?

3. What leisure activities do you do without your partner, and how does your individual leisure time affect your relationship? Does your own leisure enrich the relationship, cause tension, or balance it? Describe its effect.

4. List personality and other differences between you and your partner that sometimes cause tension in leisure choices. Next to each difference, try to write a creative way to deal with this difference.

5. List personality and other similarities between you and your partner that you can build on in your leisure choices. How can you capitalize on these similarities in planning your play?

6. In your leisure relationship, have the two of you developed specialized roles (e.g., the "social director")? How do you both feel about these roles?

7. What are several ways you can make sex more playful? Discuss this with your partner.

8. How important is play to your family life? Are you satisfied with the amount of family playtime?

9. If you have children, are there any new leisure activities you would like to share with them?

10. What are the leisure interests and general personality styles of your children? List these. Is there opportunity for each child to express his or her needs and interests?

11. Do you have a child that is hard to reach or communicate with, perhaps a teenager? What play behaviors could you try to bridge the gap?

12. How do you feel about your family vacations? What, if anything, would bring more satisfaction?

Chapter 8

Making Changes in the Work and Play Balance

As human beings, we desire change and novelty, yet we resist change because of our fear of the unknown and because of our comfort with the familiar. Many of us may talk about how wonderful it would be to change some element of our lives, but often don't follow up the talk with action. In the pages that follow, several basic approaches to change are presented that may help you effect change in your life or in the lives of others you care about.

Assertiveness

Assertiveness is an attitude and way of behaving that respects others while at the same time expresses personal beliefs, feelings, and needs. Assertiveness can be thought of as the middle ground between submissive and aggressive behavior. Submissive individuals place others in a powerful position and defer their own feelings and needs to those of others, failing to hold the same respect for themselves that they hold for others. In the face of conflict, they may withdraw, pout, cry, or simply not speak up. Aggressive individuals, on the other hand, place their own needs and opinions above everyone else's. Their behavior often reflects physical or verbal pushiness, sarcasm, and bullying. Assertive behavior includes appropriate, direct, and honest expression of opinions and feelings in a firm, respectful way. In the long run, assertive behavior brings more self-esteem, self-confidence, and respect from others and is more likely than submissive or aggressive behavior to bring desired changes.

The first step in assertive behavior is believing that we have personal rights. These include:

- the right to our own opinions

- the right to our own feelings and reactions

- the right to make mistakes

- the right to change our minds

- the right to personal privacy

Some rights are so clear-cut that we don't have to struggle with ourselves about whether we are entitled to them or not—the right to vote, for example. Rights that pertain to leisure may be less clear to many of us. Do we have the right to have fun, especially if there is still work to be done? (When is work *ever* really finished?) Here are some examples of leisure rights to think about. Do you believe you have these rights? If you give a qualified "yes," what are your conditions?

- I have the right to negotiate with my family for private time when I come home from work.

- I have the right to solitary leisure, excluding family and friends, when I need it.

- I have the right to say no when asked to do extra work that interferes with leisure plans.

- I have the right to block off time for leisure and play and to protect that time from being taken up by work or maintenance activities.

- I have the right to pursue some leisure activities that my family and friends are not interested in.

- I have the right to ask for what I need in relation to the work and play balance. (This doesn't mean that

I will always get what I ask for, but I'll never know if I don't ask!)

■ I have the right to express my own individuality through my leisure.

It is important to remember that believing you have the rights listed above, or any other rights, does *not* mean that you will always choose to assert them. There may be times that you weigh the consequences of asserting a personal right but decide not to exercise it because of negative consequences to yourself or others. The important point is awareness of such rights, of choices of behavior, and of the possible consequences. As an assertive person, you are free to make the appropriate choice for that given situation. Remember, play—by definition—involves choosing what *you* want to do.

A lack of assertiveness often leads to an unsatisfying life. You may experience some barriers to being more assertive. If someone, for example, personifies the Mother/Father archetype, she or he will have difficulty claiming many of his or her personal rights. Such people may have a self-sacrificing script that allows them only to give, but not to ask or receive. An example is the long-suffering parent who harbors subtle resentments toward the children for sacrifices made. This parent stimulates guilt in the children, but never directly asserts needs for leisure and self-development. Gender roles may also be barriers to believing in personal rights. In our culture, many of these rights can be harder for women to claim, especially if they are homemakers or mothers and feel responsible for the welfare of others or have been brought up to think of others' needs first.

Generally, Feeling types have more difficulty asserting their rights than do Thinking types. Feeling types are so concerned with harmony and pleasing others that they may defer their own rights and needs. Thinking types, on the other hand—after weighing an issue logically—may find it easier to believe they have the right to assert themselves. In general, INFP's and ISFP's seem to have the most difficulty being assertive, followed by ISFJ's. Introverts may have difficulty feeling comfortable about arranging some solitary time and leisure, especially if their family and friends are more extraverted and wish to claim their time. Whatever your type, the choice to spend time alone may be misinterpreted by others as a lack of love or as unwillingness to be involved unless you are assertive in expressing the underlying need for some solitude.

How we can express our needs and desires without alienating others? We must be able to say clearly, "I would like...," or "I need...," or "I prefer not to...." We must be able to clearly say no when a request doesn't fit our own needs and situation. Some types may have more trouble saying no than others; many Feeling types, for example, need to guard against saying yes when they really mean no. They may be able to bring themselves to say no more easily if they begin their statements with some empathetic remark that acknowledges the other person's situation: "I know there is a lot of work to do and it's important to finish it before Monday, but I've made plans to go on an outing with my son on Saturday, and this is important to me and to him. So, no, I won't be in Saturday, but maybe I can come in earlier on Friday morning." Or, "I can see you've been eager for me to get home from work so you can show me what you've done, but before you show me I need to take a few minutes to be by myself and unwind. Then I'll be ready."

Another useful technique is a *feeling assertion*. It begins with an "I feel" statement, followed by a specific emotion—such as frustrated, uncomfortable, overloaded, or excited. The statement continues with a description of the specific conditions influencing this feeling and ends with a specific request, such as "and I would like it if...."

Here are some examples of feeling assertions:

- "I'm feeling very overloaded after a hectic day in the office, and I would appreciate it if you would give me 30 minutes to myself before dinner."

- "I feel unfairly judged by you when I get ready to play tennis and you frown and say, 'Going to play tennis again?' I would like to talk about your reactions and reach some understanding, since tennis is important to me."

- "I'm feeling really frustrated that we haven't had a chance in two weeks to do any playing together. Things keep coming up and our play time seems to be a low priority. I would like to make it a higher priority. Let's sit down and figure out a way to fit in some play time together this week."

Finally, there is *assertive confrontation*, which combines elements of the feeling assertion but usually involves discussion of a recurrent problem or condition. The steps are as follows:

- Identify the problem and clarify to yourself what you feel, need, and would like.

- Approach the person when you can do so calmly and assertively, without anger or self-pity.

- Tell the person you would like to discuss something with him or her and arrange a convenient and private time.

- At the designated time, make an "I feel" statement including specific details of the recurring situation, ask for that person's perceptions of the situation, and finally ask for what you want or need.

- Allow the other person a chance to give you feedback and offer another perspective; perhaps that person has a counter-proposal, or a compromise is in order.

This approach is useful with employers who constantly ask you to work overtime and with family members and friends who don't keep promises about joining you in leisure activities. Intuitive Feeling types probably tend to be more at ease in this kind of verbal interaction. Other types may need to rehearse the steps of such a confrontation with themselves first to gain confidence to carry it out. Extraverts need to be aware that if they are confronting Introverts, they need to give some advance warning to allow them time to respond. Extraverts can make a situation worse by impatiently confronting Introverts on the spot and demanding an immediate response. Introverts, who generally need time to reflect before responding, will not be able to give their best under these conditions and may later undo an agreement they feel was made under pressure.

Assertive verbal behavior should be accompanied by congruent *nonverbal* behavior. Examples are:

- eye contact

- tone of voice

- confident body posture

- appropriate hand gestures

- appropriate facial expression

Aggressive behaviors, such as hands on the hips and a demanding tone of voice, will undermine assertive words. Similarly, submissive behaviors, such as an apologetic tone and lack of confident eye contact, will also weaken any assertive message.

Taking Responsibility

This discussion of assertiveness suggests an important principle—*taking responsibility for yourself.* This is not a selfish posture; it is an attitude of self-knowledge and awareness of what is necessary to thrive. This attitude means, "I take care of myself, so that I can then be more whole, effective, and loving with others." It also means, "I consciously choose; I am in charge of the quality of my own life." Finally, "I owe it to others, as well as to myself, to play." How can someone say they "owe it to others" to play? If play helps you to be a more balanced, satisfied individual, then you will bring more of your personal resources to your work and to your relationships. For example, an ENTJ faculty member in a major university had a heavy teaching load and supervised a large number of independent studies. It seemed there were never enough hours in the day to complete his work. Sometimes he would leave the office early to play racquetball, saying "I owe it to myself, to the students, and to my colleagues in the department to go play racquetball. I'll be more effective if I get some exercise and relax. I'll also be more pleasant!"

Positive and Negative Thinking

Another approach to change, based on concepts from Albert Ellis's *Rational Emotive Therapy* (RET) and on a type of therapy known as *cognitive restructuring*, emphasizes how our thoughts can either help or hinder us. Thinking types generally find this approach more appealing than Feeling types because it is logical and analytical. However, taking an analytical look at positive and negative thoughts complements Feeling types' natural way of looking at situations, giving them a way to balance and modify their strong subjective response.

Ellis described the ABC's of behavior this way.

A	B	C
An activating event occurs.	We tell ourselves something about that event or arrive at a belief about it.	The consequence of the event becomes clear; the belief about it generates an emotional response.

Event *A* does not *cause* the emotional response, *C*. Rather, *B*—what we tell ourselves and believe about the event—causes that emotional response. *B* is part of our regular internal chatter or narrative about the events and environment. Have you ever stopped to listen to your own internal chatter that comments on your experiences while you experience them? If this chatter becomes exaggerated or negative, our emotional responses also become negative. Here's an example. The event *A* is this: Your friend declines your invitation to go to a movie together. Negative self-talk *(B)* might go like this: "What's the use, no one wants to go out with me anyway. Why bother? Everyone has their lives scheduled already and there's no room for me in their plans." This kind of self-talk leads to discouragement and can inhibit important playfulness. Your negative thoughts are likely to prevent you from inviting others to go to films, and discourage you about your social life and self-worth in general. In this example, if you had said, "I'm disappointed; perhaps I should give this person a little more notice next time or find out ahead of time when he or she is free. I'm sure there are friends who would like to go to that movie; I just need to figure out who is free when I am and who shares my interest in film. Besides, it wouldn't be so terrible to go by myself this time if I really want to see the movie." The emotional response here is much milder and helps you encourage yourself to enjoy your leisure in other ways.

Thus, the necessary step after *C* (emotional consequence) is *D*—to dispute and modify any negative or extreme self-talk. Step *D* first calls for *developing awareness* of the self-talk that is going on. Whenever you are feeling strong negative emotions, stop and ask yourself, "What have I just said to myself that could have stimulated this strong emotional reaction?" Developing this awareness takes practice because these thoughts occur rapidly on an almost subconscious level. At first you may find yourself identifying negative self-talk after the fact, but with practice you can become better at catching yourself in the act and thus learn to modify it more quickly. The second part of step *D*, after awareness of self-talk, is *taking an objective look* at the actual situation. Try to step back and see the facts—what is known, not surmised. This is a way of challenging our subjective interpretation of an event with a more objective thought-out analysis. Extreme words, such as *always, never, should,* and *must,* can be changed to reflect a more moderate, rational perspective. Step *D* requires us to replace extreme self-talk statements with moderate, action-focused ones. In the example above, the discouraged moviegoer asks, "What's the use?" Step *D* involves substituting self-talk focused on positive actions, like finding out who may share interests and free time, or going by oneself.

Shoulds and *musts* are often obstacles to constructive change. Generally, when people act based on a *should,* they are not very motivated to either change or to maintain a change. This may be particularly true for the freedom-loving Intuitive Perceivers who don't want to be restricted by their own or others' *shoulds.* People who say they want to change will benefit from shifting their self-talk from "I *should* exercise, *should* play more with my children," and so on, to "I *want* to..." or "I *choose* to... because it is important to me." This shift may seem minor, but it is a crucial shift. It allows individuals to claim assertively what they need and to take responsibility for their own choices, instead of placing responsibility on an outside source. This shift also keeps us clearer—even more honest with ourselves—about our needs and life choices. Changes we initiate because we feel we *should* are hard to maintain, and we often feel guilty or like failures if we don't follow through on them. For example, a middle-aged man says, "I *should* run a mile and a half every day," but ends up running maybe once a week at most. He is unhappy with himself for not running and yet is not happy while running either, because he thinks of how much more he *should* be running. He would do better to talk to himself this way:

> I don't seem to be able to keep my resolution to run. Obviously, this activity is not that important or desirable to me, or I'd do it more often. What do I want for myself here? I want to be in good aerobic shape—that's really important to me at my

age. Running may not be the answer; it's boring. I think I'd like to use an exercise bicycle and watch the news on TV at the same time. I would be much more likely to follow through with it. Yes, that's what I want; it will meet my exercise needs and I'll enjoy it more.

If you cannot change your "I should" to an "I want," you may be focusing on an inappropriate choice for yourself, or one that you are not likely to consistently carry out.

Here is a simple way to practice positive self-talk to bring about change. Take a few index cards. On each card, write a negative self-statement that prevents you from playing, enjoying life, and so forth. Now cross the statement out, and on the other side of the card write the challenge (step *D*) to this negative statement. Use moderate wording and action-focused statements. You don't have to be a Pollyanna about it; don't say, "Everything will work out and life is wonderful." This may not be accurate. Just try to be rational in your statements. If you are a Feeling type, this approach may seem silly, unnatural, or even uncomfortable, but this approach can help you develop your lesser function, Thinking. In answering the question, "What do I need?" you can also exercise your Feeling preference.

Self-criticism can immobilize, or at the very least discourage, leisure attempts. Intuitive Thinking types may be so concerned with mastery of particular leisure activities that their self-talk becomes self-critical. Other types are not immune to perfectionistic thinking either—an ISTJ, for example, may give up an activity because he or she can't spend enough time at it to do it just right.

Here are some examples of the kinds of negative self-talk that are barriers to play:

- "I *should* be at such and such a standard by now; I should perform at such and such a level."

- "It would be terrible to do (an activity) alone."

- "I'll *never* get in shape, so why bother?"

- "My family *never* wants to do the things I want to do for fun, so why bother doing anything?"

- "I *must* get all my work done before I can play."

- "Adults *should* be responsible; playing is only for kids."

- "I *must never* look silly or uncoordinated in any new activity."

- "I'll *never* be a star or a high achiever at this, so what's the use?"

- "People will think I'm *foolish* for doing this."

- "I'm *selfish* to want leisure time for myself."

- "I *must always* be there for my spouse and children (or friends), otherwise I'm not a good person."

Do you recognize any of these statements? Practice becoming more aware of your ongoing internal narrative and notice how it relates to your emotional state.

Imagery

Positive mental imagery can be a useful adjunct to positive self-talk. Imagery tends to be more visual for Intuitives and more sensory or kinesthetic for Sensing types. Imagery involves using internal mental pictures or impressions, rather than statements, to motivate change and to shape positive attitudes and behavior. Imagery can be used as a mental rehearsal for a leisure activity; books such as *Inner Skiing* and *The Inner Game of Tennis* use imagery in this way to rehearse and actually improve performance. Mental rehearsal may help to carry out a new behavior or a behavior that one is reluctant to try. For instance, someone hesitant to call a friend to invite him to play might picture herself going through the steps of dialing the number, asking her friend, and receiving a positive answer. One might also rehearse not feeling discouraged if the answer is negative.

Imagery can also be used for relaxation and meditation during leisure time. Most of us have a favorite place to go to feel at peace with ourselves and to experience aesthetic beauty and tranquility. We can use that place in our mind's eye to relax and meditate. We may wish to focus on that place in meditation to contemplate the current status of balance in our lives and reflect: "How are things going for me? Do I feel in balance with myself, with others? Do I feel good about my work and my play? Is there anything missing for me now?" and so on.

Here are examples of how imagery can be useful to motivate change:

- People who want their leisure activities to satisfy physiological needs can create a visual picture of how they will look after engaging in some physical activity for a period of time. They can imagine themselves looking toned and trim. If their imagery is more sensing-oriented, they might imagine the feeling of their toned muscles, the firmness, the spring in their step, or the lightness in their bodies.

- Sensing types can also recall the sensations of a past time when they were in good shape.

- ENFP's might motivate themselves by imagining how good they will feel after completing some activity. They allow themselves to fully experience the good feeling in advance, which motivates them to want to get the real thing.

- You can imagine a time in the past when you felt particularly playful and then bring that playful feeling into the present.

- People reluctant to go out on the dance floor because they don't consider themselves good dancers could imagine themselves gliding smoothly and rhythmically and picture their body making specific moves. This mental rehearsal builds confidence and motivation to try new kinds of play.

In summarizing use of imagery, we can note differences because of personality type. Those with preferences for Intuition will more naturally motivate themselves by imagining positive future outcomes, usually using visual devices. Individuals with Sensing preferences may be more successful by recalling past impressions that were positive and motivating. Sensing types may rely more on kinesthetic impressions than on visual imagery. There seem to be some differences between Extraverts' and Introverts' use of imagery as well. Extraverts tend to close their eyes to engage in positive imagery, shutting out all distracting stimuli. However, Introverts are sometimes more successful by keeping their eyes open, since so much is going on inside for them already. Each individual needs to discover what kind of imagery works best.

The following are guided imagery experiences to try. There is one for Sensing and one for Intuition. Have someone read the directions to you as you sit or lie relaxed. Or you can make a tape recording of the directions in your own voice and play it back as you relax. Which set of directions do you prefer?

Imagery Exercises

(Read slowly; dots indicate pauses.) Lie down or sit back in a comfortable chair with your body well supported. Close your eyes and begin by noticing your breathing. Don't change it. Just observe the way the air moves in and out, in and out, the way your chest moves up and down. Take slow, deep breaths and appreciate the pause between your breath

coming in and going out, as if time were suspended between your inhaling and exhaling. Feel your arms and legs getting heavier, sinking into the chair or the floor....You are calm and relaxed. As you become more relaxed, your limbs get heavier and heavier, and your breathing gets slower and slower....

Now you are going to travel in your imagination to a specific place, a place where you experience tranquility and beauty, a place that feels perfectly safe and meant just for you.

(For Sensing Preference)
This special place may be somewhere you have been before, or somewhere you have seen in pictures, or that someone has described to you. Picture yourself traveling to this special place by car, plane, or other means....

Now you've arrived. You are very pleased to be there. Your body feels relaxed and without tension. You look around at this beautiful, peaceful scene. As you take deep breaths, you smell the air. Take time to relish the smells.... Is there a subtle fragrance to the air or a piercing freshness? Are there other smells?... Can you taste the air? Does it have a slightly salty flavor? Does it have a dry, woodsy taste found in mountain forests?

Look around you and notice specific features that make this such a lovely and peaceful place. What colors do you see? Give them delicious names, like azure blue or sparkling aquamarine. Observe the quality of the light—is it dawn, dusk? Is there any animal or plant life there? What do you see?

And what do you hear? Can you hear the wind blowing? Are there animal sounds—bird songs, the cry of a distant hawk? Are there water sounds, a babbling brook, or lapping waves? Or is there the perfect sound of silence in your peaceful place?

Can you feel the wind against your face and skin? Look down at your feet as you walk. How does the ground feel underfoot? Pick a comfortable spot to sit and peacefully enjoy the view. Experience in every part of your body the goodness and relaxation of being here....You feel the sun's warmth, giving you renewed energy. Say to yourself, "This is my special place, a place I can go whenever I need to relax and clear my thoughts."

When you've rested enough in this comfortable spot, take a last look around you and say, "I'll be back." Slowly bring your attention back to the present and your body. Gently and slowly open your eyes and sense being very refreshed and relaxed.

(For Intuitive Preference)
This place may be one where you've been before or have dreamed about. Imagine yourself now gently floating from your chair to this special place....

When you get there, look around. What do you see? Are there trees, water, rocky landscapes, or other scenery? Soak up this beautiful view. Take time to let your eyes take in everything around you.... Notice the quality of the light.

Are there any smells in your special place? What does the air smell like—dry, sweet, salty, woodsy, or what? Slowly take deep breaths, enjoying the smells and feeling totally relaxed....

Can you feel the air or the wind on your skin or perhaps the warmth of the sun?

Can you taste the air—is it salty or dry like at high altitudes, or what is it like? Does your special place evoke associations with other flavors, like the smoky taste of food cooking over a campfire?

What are the sounds around you—wind, water, birds? Or do you experience a crystalline silence? Focus your attention on the sounds around you as you continue to feel the tranquility of your special place.

As you are walking along, find a cozy spot to sit and reflect on your beautiful scene. As you settle into your spot, you feel a wave of warmth and comfort. It's wonderful to be alive. You experience a wholeness about yourself and your environment. You feel one with this place. You know you can come here whenever you wish to experience that wholeness.

When you have absorbed the energy of your special

place and feel rested, say goodbye for now, and gently float back to your body sitting in the chair here. Slowly open your eyes and savor your relaxation.

Time Management

Time management may not be the best term to describe taking responsibility for the use of time in your life, but it is a term we recognize. Some types are more open to this concept than others, yet we all want to feel like we are in charge of our lives. Judging types, especially Extraverts with dominant Judgment functions, are most at home with time management through use of schedules and plans. Perceiving types, especially the Extraverts with dominant Perception, have the most difficulty with organizing their time and setting priorities. We need to use our preferred judgment function, either Thinking or Feeling, to help us select and prioritize activities and make conscious choices about use of time. Time management is much like assertiveness and positive self-talk in helping us take responsibility for our own lives and happiness.

Judging types are more naturally able to plan their time, but this planning may focus only on work and not include necessary play. Judging types may need to plan to be spontaneous, too. This statement is a delightful paradox. Judging types can benefit from blocking off a time during the week when they will not plan, but just wait and see what happens spontaneously.

Perceiving types especially need to learn to structure their time to assure a balance of work and play. If they do not use their judgment function to select from all the perceptions gathered by their dominant perception, they will bounce from activity to activity without the satisfaction of follow-through or accomplishment. They may feel that they are in a perpetually reactive state. They may also become over-loaded by not being able to screen out activities—they don't want to miss anything, especially the Extraverts. Perceiving types may lose out on leisure opportunities that require advanced planning unless they develop some skill in managing their time.

Some find the image of a fence with a "DO NOT TRESPASS" sign around their leisure time as a useful device in time management. The leisure time blocked off this way is considered just as important as work and other obligated time. This is a way for Feeling types and Perceiving types especially to increase the likelihood that they really will get to play or relax. However, one must believe one has the right to have time for oneself in order to do necessary planning and implementation. Fencing off time may be done on a daily basis or several times a week. Some types will enjoy planning each day; others will take a more general, less detailed approach. The needs of the types vary, making it difficult to recommend one time management approach. The point is that the types most reluctant to schedule do need to practice at least some broad-brush or general planning to assure time for leisure as well as work.

Besides type considerations, one might wish to consider daily rhythms and energy levels. Some people are early risers who enjoy jogging or other early-morning leisure activity. They then feel assured that they have already accomplished their leisure activity and don't spend the day wondering if there will be time or motivation. Others look forward to leisure at the end of the day as a time to unwind or reward themselves. Some busy dual-career families squeeze leisure activities into lunch hours and on the way home from work. It is a challenge to fit leisure into family schedules, especially if there are young children. Planning may have to be especially creative.

Periodic self-evaluation of your daily activity pattern and balance is important. Meditation can be a vehicle for self-examination of emotional and mental status, needs, and so on. Because needs vary from time to time, the same plan or approach will not work indefinitely. We need to remain flexible and sensitive to conditions in ourselves and in our surroundings. Some people find keeping a journal to be helpful in self-evaluation. By writing down their thoughts and feelings they become clearer about what they need in the way of balance at any given time. They can use writing to clarify personal rights, self-talk, and choices. Others, especially Extraverts, find talking to a friend or family member helpful in evaluating themselves. Someone else can often give us another perspective, especially if their personality type is different from ours. When people become particularly unhappy or dissatisfied and are unable to change on their own, they may consider seeking help from a professional counselor, psychologist, minister, or other helping person.

Learning from Other Types

Sometimes we see others we admire and say to ourselves, "I'd like to be like that." "That person really has her act together!" "I wish I could be as playful or have as much fun as he does." Look around. Are there qualities in others you would like to emulate in balancing your work and play? By observing how they do it and imitating their behavior, you can make an admired quality your own with practice. You can even ask your role models how they manage to do it. Discuss with them specifically how they accomplish the behavior you admire.

If you are trying to develop your lesser functions, finding models with those functions dominant is helpful. For example, a Feeling type having difficulty learning to be assertive about private time might talk the situation over with a Thinking type. The Thinking type might explain how he or she handles that kind of situation assertively. A Feeling type might explain to a Thinking type how to make guests feel comfortable and at ease. An individual with a Sensing preference might learn from an Intuitive person how to bring imagination into play; the Intuitive friend might suggest new leisure activities. Sensing types can help dominant Intuitives learn to stop and smell the roses. Judging types and Perceiving types can show each other how to be organized and flexible. Less developed functions can be developed by practice, even though at first it may only feel like acting. It takes time to incorporate new behavior into our repertoire.

Particularly rich modeling can occur if you can observe someone of the same type as you but at least ten years older. You will probably observe many familiar characteristics as well as some subtle differences. The older person may present a model of how it looks to develop the lesser preferences, or temper the extremes of the dominant ones.

Some Final Comments on Change

Staying in Touch with Your Child Within

Many of us lose touch with our own internal, natural child as we become adults. This is the part of ourselves that allows us to enjoy life without inhibition, to be creative, and to see the world through unjaded, wondering eyes. We all have the ability to rediscover our inner child and make it a part of healthy, adult living. Think of this as the energetic, creative, spontaneous part of yourself. Imagery can be one way to get in touch with your inner child. Another way is to spend some time with young children, watching them play and trying to imitate their attitudes in your own modified adult way. Try to see the world the way children see it. Try to reserve your adult judgment about the way things are supposed to be, letting yourself experience the world in a fresh way—as if it were the first time. For example, take a toddler to the beach and act as if you've never seen a sea gull or a sand crab before; discover these things with the child. These attitudes can be transferred to your leisure and lifestyle as a whole. The point is not to conduct business in a *childish* way but rather to retain the *childlike* naturalness of being playful when appropriate.

Humor

Humor is a wonderful and legitimate way for adults to be playful and to make contact with each other. It is a special form of communication. Some people are skilled at telling "canned" jokes, while others may not even be able to remember jokes in the correct sequence. Other people are able to see the inherent humor in a given situation and make amusing comments.

Humor can help us maintain balance in our lives. The ability to laugh at ourselves helps us transcend a situation and see it from a different perspective. In order to laugh, we must shift our viewpoint from being actor to audience, and in so doing gain a novel perspective and some freedom from the tension of the original situation. We can laugh at our exaggerated negative thinking, or we can deliberately exaggerate our self-talk until we see its absurdity; this frees us to change to more positive self-talk. Humor is a way to lighten up and put things in perspective; the result can be permission to enjoy ourselves even when our world isn't completely right. Finally, humor at an appropriate time and place encourages reciprocal playful responses in others and thus generates a play-supporting environment. Work often becomes play when appropriate humor is included.

The Spiritual Glue

The word *spiritual* has varying meaning to different people and types. Many Sensing and Judging types think of *spiritual* as meaning religious in the traditional sense. Many Intuitive and Perceiving types think of *spiritual* in a more philosophical sense, one that is more personal and less tied to social traditions. For all of us the word *spiritual* suggests some kind of belief in a higher power and a belief about the meaning of our lives. We all need a sense of meaning and purpose as well as a sense of belonging to something greater than ourselves; Jung used the term *collective unconscious*. This spiritual sense can be thought of as the glue that holds the individual or self together.

Early in this book, Jung's theory of type development suggested that the development and expression of the least preferred third and fourth functions often had a spiritual quality. At midlife, spiritual issues take on new meaning as individuals search for something beyond their own immediate existences. Leisure can also provide opportunities for exploration of the lesser functions, which may lead to transforming experiences. Csikszentmihalyi's flow experience was also considered as a spiritual path of sorts. Different types may seek varying forms of worship, meditation, and spiritual exploration, especially at midlife. It is important for us to nourish the spiritual part of ourselves in the way most appropriate to our needs and personality preferences. This spiritual dimension incorporates parts of ourselves formerly unconscious and brings us into closer touch with our larger self, beyond that of our dominant and auxiliary, or preferred, functions. In so doing this spiritually expanded self has more resources with which to bring about balance and satisfaction.

Think About ...

1. Under what circumstances is it difficult for you to be assertive about your needs?

2. What specific personal rights do you believe you have in relation to leisure?

3. Are there some personal rights you doubt? If so, which? What could you do to resolve your doubt?

4. How could you use an empathetic assertion to say no about something specific in your life?

5. What is an example of a feeling assertion applied to some aspect of your life?

6. Is there an ongoing situation related to work or play that you would like to address using a confrontation assertion? Describe.

7. What, if any, negative thoughts sometimes interfere with your playing? List them. Now write a positive modification to each of these negative thoughts.

8. What imagery have you found helpful in motivating you to change your behavior? How can you further develop positive imagery to help you?

9. What is your attitude toward time management? What is a comfortable and effective approach for you?

10. Who are some very different personalities or psychological types that you can learn from, perhaps by imitating behavior that you admire?

11. How do you get in touch with your natural child? Do you want your inner child to be more present in your adult life? If so, how?

12. How much is humor a part of your life, and how could you further enhance your life with humor?

13. How do you express your spiritual self? Are their opportunities you could pursue in the spiritual area?

Notes

Chapter 1
1. Harris Poll, *Orlando Sentinel*, Sept. 17, 1988.
2. Csikszentmihalyi, M. (1975). *Beyond boredom and anxiety: The experience of play in work and games* (p. 4). San Francisco: Jossey-Bass.

Chapter 3
3. Ibid, p. 36.
4. Ibid, p. 24.
5. Ibid, p. 30.
6. Rohbaugh, J.B. (1979). Femininity on the line. *Psychology Today, 13,* (3), 44.

Chapter 4
7. Ragheb, M. G., & Beard, J. G. (1980). Leisure satisfaction, concept theory, and measurement. In S. E. Iso-Ahola (Ed.), *Social psychological perspectives on leisure and recreation.* Springfield, IL: Charles C. Thomas.

Chapter 6
8. Rubenstein, C. (1980). Survey report: How Americans view vacations. *Psychology Today, 13,* (12), 62–77.
9. Ibid, p. 76.

Further Readings

Alberti, R., & Emmons, M. (1970). *Your perfect right: A guide to assertive behavior*. San Luis Obispo, CA: Impact Books.

Bischoff, L. J. (1969). *Adult psychology*. New York: Harper & Row.

Bolles, R. N. (1978). *The three boxes of life*. Berkeley, CA: Ten Speed Press.

Campbell, J. (Ed.). (1971). *The portable Jung*. New York: Penguin Books.

Campbell, J., & Moyers, B. (1988). *The power of myths*. New York: Doubleday.

Castenada, C. (1971). *A separate reality*. New York: Simon & Schuster.

Castenada, C. (1972). *Journey to Ixtlan*. New York: Simon & Schuster.

Castenada, C. (1974). *Tales of power*. New York: Simon & Schuster.

Ellis, A., & Harper, R. (1975). *A guide to rational living*. North Hollywood, CA: Wilshire Book Co.

Ellis, M. J. (1973). *Why people play*. Englewood Cliffs, NJ: Prentice Hall.

Erikson, E. (1968). *Identity: Youth and crisis*. New York: Norton.

Galloway, W. T. (1974). *The inner game of tennis*. New York: Bantam.

Galloway, W. T., & Kriegel, R. (1977). *Inner skiing*. New York: Bantam.

Guzie, T., & Guzie, N. (1986). *About men and women*. New York: Paulist Press.

Havighurst, R. J. (1972). *Developmental tasks and education*. New York: David McKay.

Johannes, T. B., & Bull, C. N. (Eds.). (1971). *Sociology of leisure.* Beverly Hills, CA: Sage.

Jung, C. G. (1923). *Psychological types.* New York: Harcourt Brace Jovanovich.

Keirsey, D., & Bates, M. (1984). *Please understand me.* Del Mar, CA: Promethean Books.

Lange, A., & Jakubowski, P. (1976). *Responsible assertive behavior.* Champaign, IL: Research Press.

LeShan, L. (1974). *How to meditate.* New York: Bantam.

Murphy, J. F. (1975). *Recreation and leisure services: A humanistic perspective.* Dubuque, IA: William Brown.

Myers, I. (1980). *Gifts differing.* Palo Alto, CA: Consulting Psychologists Press.

Myers, I., & McCaulley, M. (1987). *Manual: A guide to the development and use of the Myers-Briggs Type Indicator.* Palo Alto, CA: Consulting Psychologists Press.

Neulinger, J. (1974). *The psychology of leisure: Research approaches to the study of leisure.* Springfield, IL: Charles C. Thomas.

Pearson, C. (1986). *The hero within.* San Francisco: Harper & Row.

Provost, J. (1984). *A casebook: Applications of the Myers-Briggs Type Indicator in counseling.* Gainesville, FL: CAPT.

Provost, J., & Anchors, S. (Eds.). (1987). *Applications of the Myers-Briggs Type Indicator in higher education.* Palo Alto, CA: Consulting Psychologists Press.

Provost, J. (1988). *Procrastination.* Gainesville, FL: CAPT.

Weber, M. (1930). *The Protestant ethic and the spirit of capitalism.* London: Allen & Unwin.

About the Author

Dr. Provost is currently Director of Counseling and Health Services at Rollins College. She received her doctorate in counselor education from the University of Florida and a masters degree from UCLA. In addition to her work as a psychotherapist, she is a consultant and national trainer for the *Myers-Briggs Type Indicator* (MBTI). She lives with her husband, Steven, in Central Florida. They have two daughters. Type has proven valuable to their family life, especially in learning to appreciate differences—Judy's preferences are ENFP, whereas Steven's are ESTJ. Play activities that Judy has found to enrich and balance her professional life include tennis, aerobics, volleyball, sailing, canoeing, reading, attending films, and dancing.